Family Circle

HOME BAKING

Albany Books

Designed and produced by
Albany Books
36 Park Street London W1Y 4DE

First published 1979

Published by Albany Books

Copyright © Albany Books 1979

Printed in Hong Kong

ISBN 0 86136 085 0

*This text has previously been
published in issues of* Family Circle.
*The publishers wish to thank the
Editor and staff of the magazine for
their help in preparing it for this
edition. They also gratefully
acknowledge the loan of
transparencies from* Family Circle.

*Design : Walker Pinfold Associates
Picture Research : Raj Sacranie*

The recipes contain both metric
and imperial measurements: these
are not always exact equivalents,
so do not mix them up.

Contents

Cooking with Yeast

WHITE BREAD

Yeast Liquid
1 × 5ml spoon (1 level teaspoon) castor sugar
125ml (¼ pint) hand-hot water
1 × 15ml spoon (1 level tablespoon) dried yeast

Dough
1½kg (3lb) plain flour
2 × 15ml spoons (2 level tablespoons) salt
25g (1oz) lard

1. Dissolve castor sugar in hand-hot water; sprinkle dried yeast over and leave until frothy, about 10 minutes.
2. Place flour and salt in a bowl.

Add lard, cut into small pieces, and rub in with the fingertips until mixture resembles fine bread-crumbs. Mix in yeast liquid and a scant 700ml (1½ pints) water with a wooden spoon and the hands, adding extra flour, if needed, until dough leaves side of bowl.
3. Turn out dough on to a floured board. Knead and stretch dough by folding towards you, then pushing away with the palm of the hand. Give dough a quarter turn and repeat, developing a rocking motion. Knead for about 10 minutes until dough feels firm and no longer sticky.
4. Place dough in a bowl, cover with greased polythene and leave to rise until doubled in size, about 1 hour. Test by pressing with a

floured finger, when dough should spring back.
5. Turn out dough on to a floured board and knead to disperse any large air bubbles. Shape, as desired (see below). Prepare a hot oven (230 deg C, 450 deg F, Gas Mark 8).

Note : Alternatively, use fresh yeast; blend 25g (1oz) yeast with 125ml (¼ pint) warm water (omit sugar) and use at once.

BROWN BREAD

Yeast Liquid
1 × 5ml (1 level teaspoon) castor sugar
125ml (¼ pint) hand-hot water (40 deg C, 110 deg F)
1½ × 15ml spoons (1½ level tablespoons) dried yeast

Dough
1kg (2lb) plain wholemeal or wholewheat flour
½kg (1lb) plain flour
2 × 5ml spoons (2 level tablespoons) salt
2 × 5ml spoons (2 level tablespoons) castor sugar
50g (2oz) lard

1. Dissolve 1 × 5ml spoon (1 level teaspoon) castor sugar in hand-hot water. Sprinkle dried yeast on top and leave until frothy, about 10 minutes.
2. Place flours, salt and 2 × 15ml spoons (2 level tablespoons) castor sugar in a large bowl. Add lard, cut

Left: Tin loaf, plait loaf, baps and rolls made from brown bread

into small pieces, and rub in with the fingertips until mixture resembles fine breadcrumbs. Mix in yeast liquid and 900ml (1½ pints) water (warm, if you are in a hurry). Mix with a wooden spoon, adding a little extra flour, if needed, until dough leaves sides of bowl.
3. Turn out dough on to a floured board; shape as desired (see below). Cover with greased polythene and leave to rise until doubled in size, about 1 hour.
4. Prepare a hot oven (230 deg C, 450 deg F, Gas Mark 8). Remove polythene; bake bread in centre of oven for 25 to 30 minutes. To test: Remove loaf from baking sheet or tin; tap base. If cooked, loaf will sound hollow. Leave to cool on a wire rack.

Note : Alternatively, use 50g (1½oz) fresh yeast in place of 1½ × 15ml spoons (1½ tablespoons) dried yeast; use warm water in place of hand-hot.

To make a tin loaf: Use a quarter of dough for a ½kg (1lb) loaf; half of dough for a 1kg (2lb)

loaf. Flatten piece of dough to the width of the base of tin and 3 times as long. Fold into 3; place in greased tin, smooth side upper-most. Place in a greased polythene bag. Leave to rise to top of tin, about 1 hour; remove bag. Place on a baking sheet and bake in centre of oven for 30 to 35 minutes.

To make a cob or bap loaf: Use a sixth of dough. Knead piece of dough to a ball; press down to flatten and place on a floured baking sheet. Cover with greased polythene and leave to rise until doubled in size, about 1 hour; remove polythene. Bake in centre of oven for 25 to 30 minutes.

To make a plait loaf: Use a sixth of dough. Divide piece of dough into 3; roll each piece with the hands into a long roll. Gather together one end of each; plait rolls. Place on a greased baking sheet, cover with greased poly-thene and leave to rise until doubled in size, about 1 hour; remove polythene. Bake in centre of oven for 25 to 30 minutes.

Left: *Breads, teabreads and pizza—all made with short-time bread dough*

bread, use 15 fluid oz warm water and wholemeal flour instead of white flour.)

To Make a Tin Loaf

Grease a $\frac{1}{2}$kg (1lb) loaf tin. Use half quantity of dough; flatten to the width of base of tin and 3 times the length. Fold into 3 and place in tin, smooth side uppermost. Place in a greased polythene bag and leave to rise to top of tin, about 30 minutes. Remove polythene and brush loaf with beaten egg or milk, to glaze. Bake loaf in centre of oven for 20 to 25 minutes. To test: Remove loaf from tin and tap base. If cooked, loaf will sound hollow. Leave to cool on a wire rack.

To Make Rolls

Grease a baking sheet. Use half quantity of dough; divide into 12 pieces.

Plait Rolls: Divide one piece of dough into 3. Roll each piece with the hands into a roll, about 10cm (4in) long. Press together at one end of each; plait rolls. Place on baking sheet.

Knot Rolls: Roll out one piece of dough with the hands into a roll, about 15cm (6in) long. Loosely tie into a knot and place on baking sheet.

Cottage Rolls: Cut off one-third of one piece of dough. Shape each of the two pieces into a ball. Place larger piece on baking sheet and smaller piece on top. Press a floured wooden-spoon handle through centre of both rounds, from the top.

Round Rolls: Place a little flour on the palm of the hand, press down on a piece of dough, hard at first, then roll dough in a circular movement, gradually easing up palm of hand. Cover rolls with greased polythene and leave to rise until doubled in size. Remove polythene; brush rolls with beaten egg or milk, to glaze. Bake in centre of oven for 10 to 15 minutes.

BASIC SHORT-TIME BREAD DOUGH

Yeast Liquid
25g (1oz) fresh yeast
350ml (14 fluid oz) warm water
1 (25mg) ascorbic acid tablet
1kg (1$\frac{1}{2}$lb) strong plain flour
1×15ml spoon (1 level tablespoon) salt
1×5ml spoon (1 level teaspoon) castor sugar
25g ($\frac{1}{2}$oz) lard

1. Crumble yeast into water in a measuring jug; add ascorbic acid tablet and whisk with a fork until dissolved.
2. Place flour, salt and sugar in a bowl. Add lard, cut into small pieces, and rub in with the finger-tips until mixture resembles fine breadcrumbs.
3. Add yeast liquid; mix, adding extra flour, if necessary, until dough leaves side of bowl.
4. Turn out dough on to a floured board. Knead and stretch dough, by folding towards you, then pushing away with the palm of the hand. Give dough a quarter turn and repeat, developing a rocking motion. Knead for about 10 minutes, until dough feels firm, elastic and no longer sticky.
5. Shape into a ball; replace in bowl. Cover with polythene and leave for 5 minutes.
6. Prepare a hot oven (230 deg C, 450 deg F, Gas Mark 8). Shape dough as desired (see instructions below).

Note: If using a mixer, prepare yeast liquid in mixer bowl and add dry ingredients. Mix with dough hook at speed 1 for 1 minute, then increase to speed 3 and mix for a further 3 minutes. Shape dough into a ball; replace in mixer bowl. Cover with polythene; leave for 5 minutes. (If strong plain flour is not available, use a good quality plain flour and reduce water to 13 fluid oz. To make wholemeal

Buns, Teabreads and Scones

SHORT-TIME ENRICHED DOUGH

Yeast Liquid
25g (1oz) fresh yeast
225ml (8 fluid oz) warm milk
1 (25mg) ascorbic acid tablet

Dough
450g (1lb) strong plain flour
1×5ml spoon (1 level teaspoon) salt
1×5ml spoon (1 level teaspoon) castor sugar
50g (2oz) margarine
1 egg, beaten

1. Crumble yeast into milk in a jug; add ascorbic acid tablet, whisk with a fork until dissolved.
2. Place flour, salt and sugar in a bowl. Add margarine, cut into small pieces, and rub in with the fingertips until mixture resembles fine breadcrumbs. Add yeast liquid and beaten egg; mix with a fork and the hands to form a soft dough.
3. Turn out on to a floured board. Knead and stretch dough by folding towards you, then pushing away with the palm of the hand. Give dough a quarter turn and repeat, using a rocking motion. Knead for about 10 minutes until dough feels firm and elastic and is no longer sticky.
4. Replace dough in bowl, cover with greased polythene and leave for 10 minutes. Knead for 2 minutes; use immediately.

Note: If using a mixer, prepare yeast liquid in mixer bowl. Add rubbed-in mixture to yeast liquid, with beaten egg. Mix with dough hook at speed 1 for 1 minute; increase speed to 3 and mix for 3 minutes. Shape dough into a ball; replace in mixer bowl. Cover with greased polythene, leave for 10 minutes, knead again. Dried yeast can be used but, as it takes about one hour longer to rise, the quick-rise advantage is lost.

HOT CROSS BUNS

Castor sugar
1×5ml spoon (1 level teaspoon) mixed spice
1×5ml spoon (1 tablespoon) hot water
Half quantity short time enriched dough
25g (1oz) currants
25g (1oz) mixed peel

Glaze
1×15ml spoon (1 tablespoon) milk

1. Brush a baking sheet with melted fat or oil. Place 25g (1oz) castor sugar and mixed spice in a basin, add hot water and mix together until the sugar has completely dissolved.
2. Place dough on a lightly floured board; knead sugar mixture, currants and mixed peel into dough until evenly distributed; sprinkle lightly with flour if the dough becomes sticky and then continue kneading.
3. Form dough into an oblong and cut into 10 even-sized pieces. Shape each piece into a ball with the fingertips. Place on baking sheet and flatten slightly. Place 1×15ml spoon (1 tablespoon) castor sugar and milk in a small saucepan. Heat pan gently, until the sugar has dissolved. Brush buns all over with half the glaze.
4. Mark crosses on buns with a sharp knife. Cover loosely with greased polythene and leave in a warm place for 30 minutes or until each bun has doubled in size.
5. Meanwhile, prepare a hot oven (220 deg C, 425 deg F, Gas Mark 7). Remove polythene and bake buns in centre of oven for 10 to 12 minutes until golden brown. Remove from oven and place on a wire rack. Brush the buns with remaining glaze while they are still hot.
6. To serve warm: Place buns in a roasting tin. Cover with foil or a lid and heat in a cool oven (150 deg C, 300 deg F, Gas Mark 2) for 15 minutes. Alternatively, place in grill pan and heat under a low grill, turning the buns once.

Note: If using a mixer, place dough in mixer bowl, add sugar mixture, currants and mixed peel to bowl and mix with dough hook at speed 2 for 1 minute.

DOUGHNUTS
Makes 8

Half quantity short-time enriched
 dough
Raspberry jam
Oil or fat for deep frying
50g (2oz) castor sugar
1 × 2·5ml spoon (½ level teaspoon)
 cinnamon

---

1. Divide dough into 8 pieces.
Place a little jam in the middle of
each piece; shape into doughnuts.
2. Place doughnuts in greased
patty tins or on a baking sheet.
Cover with greased polythene and
leave in a warm place for 30
minutes, or until dough has
doubled in size. Remove polythene.
3. Heat a pan of oil or fat to 188
deg C (370 deg F), or until a
2·5cm (1in) cube of day-old bread
browns in 40 seconds.
4. Fry doughnuts for 4 minutes.
Remove from pan, drain on kitchen
paper, then roll in sugar and
cinnamon. Leave until cold.

Right: Doughnuts

CHELSEA BUNS
Makes 9

Half quantity short-time enriched
 dough
50g (2oz) butter, softened
50g (2oz) brown sugar
25g (1oz) sultanas
25g (1oz) cut mixed peel
Golden syrup to glaze

---

1. Roll out dough on a lightly
floured board to an oblong, 30cm
by 23cm (12in by 9in).
2. Spread dough with butter.
Sprinkle with sugar, fruit and peel.
Roll up from the long side, like a
Swiss roll, and seal edges.
3. Cut into 9 equal pieces. Arrange
8 pieces, cut sides downwards, in
a circle on a lightly-greased baking
sheet; place remaining piece in the
centre. Place baking sheet in a
large, greased polythene bag and
leave in a warm place for 30
minutes, or until dough has
doubled in size.
4. Prepare a moderate oven (190
deg C, 375 deg F, Gas Mark 5).
Remove the polythene bag; bake
in centre of oven for 30 minutes.
Remove from oven and brush with
golden syrup. Cool on a wire rack.

Note: Alternatively, place in a
greased, deep 20·5cm (8in) square
cake tin.

Left: Chelsea buns

DEVONSHIRE SPLITS
Makes 12

Yeast Liquid

1 × 5ml spoon (1 level teaspoon)
castor sugar

250ml (½ pint) hand-hot milk,
40 deg C (110 deg F)

1 × 15ml spoon (1 level tablespoon)
dried yeast

Dough

50g (2oz) margarine

450g (1lb) strong plain flour

50g (2oz) castor sugar

1 × 5ml spoon (1 level teaspoon)
salt

Filling

1 170ml (6 fluid oz) carton
double cream

2 × 15ml spoon (2 tablespoons)
milk

Strawberry jam

Icing sugar

1. Dissolve 5ml (1 level teaspoon)
castor sugar in the milk in a small

basin; sprinkle on yeast and leave
until frothy, about 10 minutes.
2. Melt margarine in a small
saucepan; leave to cool. Place
flour, 50g (2oz) castor sugar and
salt in a bowl; add margarine and
yeast liquid and mix to a fairly stiff
dough.
3. Turn out dough on to a floured
board and knead and stretch dough
by folding towards you, then pushing away with the palm of the hand.
Give dough a quarter turn and repeat, developing a rocking motion.
Knead for about 10 minutes, until
dough feels firm and elastic.
4. Place dough in a bowl; cover
with greased polythene and leave
to rise in a warm place, until
doubled in size and dough springs
back when pressed with a floured
finger (45 minutes to 1 hour).
5. Turn out dough on to a floured
board and knead lightly. Divide
dough into 12 equal pieces; shape
each piece into a round bun with
the fingertips. Place on a greased

Above: *Devonshire splits*

baking sheet; cover with greased
polythene. Leave to rise in a warm
place for 25 to 30 minutes.
6. Prepare a hot oven (230 deg C,
450 deg F, Gas Mark 8).
7. Remove polythene and cook
buns in centre of oven for 10 to 12
minutes, until golden brown.
Leave to cool on a wire rack.
8. Place cream and milk in a bowl;
whisk until just thick. Make a cut in
each bun with a sharp knife, from
one side of top diagonally through
to centre. Open out each bun and
spread one half of each with jam
and the other with cream. Alternatively, fill buns with 225g (½lb)
clotted cream. Place a little icing
sugar in a sieve, hold over buns and
tap lightly, to sift a little over each.

Note: Alternatively, use fresh
yeast: Blend 25g (1oz) with
measured amount of warm milk
(omit sugar): use at once.

APPLE DOUGH CAKE

Half quantity short-time enriched
  dough

Filling

75g (3oz) lard
2×15ml spoons (1 rounded
  tablespoon) brown sugar
1×15ml spoon (1 level
  tablespoon) golden syrup
1×2·5ml spoon (½ level teaspoon)
  mixed spice
1 small cooking apple
75g (3oz) sultanas

1. Lightly brush a deep, round
18cm (7in) cake tin with melted fat.
Cut lard into pieces and arrange
over base of tin; sprinkle with
brown sugar. Measure golden
syrup carefully, levelling off spoon
with a knife and making sure there
is none on underside of spoon.
Drizzle over lard in cake tin.
2. Peel, core and coarsely chop
apple. Turn out dough on to a
floured board. Knead mixed spice,
sultanas and apple into dough
until evenly distributed; sprinkle
with flour if dough becomes sticky.
3. Press dough into prepared cake
tin; place tin in a greased polythene
bag; leave in a warm place until
the dough has doubled in size—
about 30 minutes. Meanwhile,
prepare a moderate oven (200
deg C, 400 deg F, Gas Mark 6.)
4. Remove polythene bag and
bake in centre of oven for 30 to 35
minutes; invert and leave to cool
completely on a wire rack. Alternatively, the cake may be served hot
from the oven with custard or
fresh cream for a delicious pudding.

Right, clockwise from top: *Apple dough
cake, orange and lemon whirly, spicy
apple teabread, cherry bubble loaf*

ORANGE AND LEMON WHIRLY

1 quantity short-time
  enriched dough

Filling
1 medium-sized orange
25g (1oz) soft brown sugar
1 × 10ml spoon (1 rounded
  teaspoon) nutmeg

Beaten egg or milk to glaze

Glacé Icing
100g (4oz) icing sugar
Juice from orange

Decoration
2 orange jelly slices
2 lemon jelly slices

1. Brush 1kg (2lb) loaf tin with melted fat. Scrub orange, grate rind, squeeze juice and reserve. Place rind in a small basin; add remaining filling ingredients and mix together.
2. Place dough on a floured board and knead lightly. Roll out to an oblong 38cm by 16·5cm (15in by 6½in). Brush off surplus flour. Brush dough lightly with water and spread filling over surface to within 2cm (½in) of edges.
3. Roll up Swiss roll fashion and place with join downwards in prepared tin. Place tin in a greased polythene bag and leave in a warm place until dough has doubled in size—about 30 minutes.
4. Meanwhile, prepare a moderately hot oven (200 deg C, 400 deg F, Gas Mark 6). Remove bag from loaf; brush top with beaten egg or milk. Bake loaf in centre of oven for 30 to 35 minutes until loaf is well risen and has begun to shrink from sides of tin. Remove from tin and leave to cool.
5. To make glacé icing: sift icing sugar into a basin and add sufficient reserved orange juice to make the icing the consistency of thick cream. Using a teaspoon, run icing over top of loaf to coat. Decorate loaf with quartered jelly slices.

CHERRY BUBBLE LOAF

Half quantity short-time enriched dough

Filling
100g (4oz) glacé cherries
50g (2oz) shelled hazelnuts
50g (2oz) brown sugar
Milk to glaze

1. Brush a 500g (1lb) loaf tin with melted fat. Cut glacé cherries into quarters. Chop hazelnuts coarsely and mix with brown sugar.
2. Place dough on a floured board, knead lightly and form into an oblong. Cut into 22 even-sized pieces. Roll each piece into a ball; flatten each ball with the palm of the hand. Place some quartered cherries in the centre of each. Bring up dough to cover glacé cherries and form a ball. Repeat with remaining dough balls and cherries.
3. Place 11 balls in prepared loaf tin, sprinkle with half the hazelnuts and sugar mixture. Arrange remaining balls in the spaces; sprinkle with remaining nuts and sugar.
4. Place in a greased polythene bag and leave in a warm place to rise until doubled in size—about 30 minutes. Meanwhile, prepare a hot oven (220 deg 3, 425 deg F, Gas Mark 7).
5. Remove bag from loaf; brush top with milk. Bake loaf in centre of oven for 20 to 25 minutes until risen and golden brown. Leave to cool in tin for 5 minutes. Run a knife between loaf and tin, turn out and leave to cool completely on a wire rack. Serve sliced and buttered or break off balls and eat individually.

SPICY APPLE TEABREAD

1 large cooking apple
50g (2oz) butter
300g (12oz) self-raising flour
½ × 2·5ml spoon (¼ level teaspoon) salt
1 × 5ml spoon (1 level teaspoon) ground allspice
1 × 2·5ml spoon (½ level teaspoon) ground nutmeg
1 × 5ml spoon (1 level teaspoon) mixed spice
75g (3oz) soft brown sugar (dark)
3 eggs
75g (3oz) sultanas

1. Prepare a cool oven (170 deg C, 325 deg F, Gas Mark 3). Brush a 1kg (2lb) loaf tin with melted fat. Peel, core and grate apple.
2. Place butter in a small saucepan; heat gently until butter has melted, remove from heat, allow to cool.
3. Sift flour, salt, allspice, nutmeg and mixed spice into a bowl; add brown sugar. Beat eggs together, make a 'well' in dry ingredients and add beaten eggs with melted butter.
4. Mix well, then stir in grated apple and sultanas.
5. Pour mixture into prepared tin; level top with back of spoon. Bake in centre of oven for 1 to 1½ hours until loaf is well risen and has begun to shrink from sides of tin. Leave to cool in tin for 5 minutes.

Turn out and leave to cool completely on a wire rack. Serve sliced and buttered.

Note: This loaf will improve in flavour if stored for up to 2 weeks in a tin.

BARA BRITH

Yeast Batter
125g (5oz) plain flour
1 × 5ml spoon (1 level teaspoon) castor sugar
1 × 15ml spoon (1 level tablespoon) dried yeast
200ml (8 fluid oz) hand-hot milk 40 deg C (110 deg F)

Dough
275g (11oz) plain flour
50g (2oz) lard
1 egg
1 × 5ml spoon (1 level teaspoon) salt
50g (2oz) soft brown sugar (light)
1 × 2·5ml spoon (½ level teaspoon) mixed spice
75g (3oz) raisins
75g (3oz) currants
75g (3oz) sultanas
25g (1oz) cut mixed peel

1. Grease a 1kg (2lb) loaf tin.
2. Place batter ingredients in a large bowl. Beat well with a wooden spoon until smooth; set aside in a warm place until frothy, about 20 minutes.
3. Place 275g (11oz) plain flour in a bowl. Add lard, cut into small pieces, and rub in with the fingertips until mixture resembles fine breadcrumbs. Beat egg and salt together in a small basin.
4. Add rubbed-in mixture, egg, sugar, mixed spice, raisins, currants, sultanas and cut mixed peel to batter. Mix well with a wooden spoon or with the hands. Turn out on to a lightly-floured board. Knead and stretch dough by folding towards you, then pushing away with the palm of the hand. Give dough a quarter turn and repeat, developing a rocking motion. Knead for about 10 minutes, until dough feels firm and elastic and no longer sticky.
5. Place dough in a lightly-floured bowl or saucepan. Cover with greased polythene, foil or a lid. Leave to rise for about 1 hour, or until dough has doubled in size and will spring back when pressed with a floured finger.
6. Turn out dough on to lightly-floured board and knead. Flatten dough to the width of base of tin and 3 times as long. Fold in 3, turn over and place in tin. Cover with greased polythene or foil and leave until dough rises to the top of tin.
7. Prepare a moderate oven (190 deg C, 375 deg F, Gas Mark 5). Remove cover from tin and bake loaf in centre of oven for ¾ to 1 hour, or until it shrinks slightly from sides of tin and crust is deep golden brown. To test: Turn loaf out of tin and tap base. If cooked, loaf will sound hollow. Leave to cool on a wire rack. Serve sliced and buttered.

Note: Alternatively, use 25g (1oz) fresh yeast in place of 1 × 15ml spoon (1 tablespoon) dried yeast; use warm milk in place of hand-hot milk.

Right, clockwise from top: *Bara brith, Sally Lunn, butter whirls, muffins*

SALLY LUNN

Yeast Batter
75g (3oz) plain flour
1 × 5ml spoon (1 level teaspoon) castor sugar
125ml (¼ pint), plus 3 × 15ml spoons (3 tablespoons) hand-hot milk

Dough
150g (6oz) plain flour
1 × 5ml spoon (1 level teaspoon) salt
1 × 5ml spoon (1 level teaspoon) mixed spice
25g (1oz) castor sugar
25g (1oz) butter, melted
1 egg

1. Brush a 15cm (6in) deep round cake tin with melted fat. Line base and side with greaseproof paper; grease paper.
2. Place batter ingredients in a large bowl. Beat well with a wooden spoon until smooth; leave in a warm place until frothy, about 20 minutes.
3. Add dough ingredients to batter; beat with a wooden spoon until smooth. Pour into tin; cover tin with polythene or foil. Leave to rise until doubled in size.
4. Prepare a hot oven (220 deg C, 425 deg F, Gas Mark 7). Remove polythene or foil. Place tin on shelf below centre of oven and bake for 35 minutes, until golden brown. If top becomes too brown before end of cooking time, cover with grease-proof paper. Remove from tin; leave to cool on a wire rack. Serve warm or cold, cut into slices and buttered.

Note : Alternatively, use 25g (½oz) fresh yeast in place of 2 × 5ml spoons (2 teaspoons) dried yeast; use warm milk in place of hand-hot.

BUTTER WHIRLS
Makes 9

125g (5oz) butter
200g (8oz) self-raising flour
Scant 125ml (¼ pint) milk
4 × 15ml spoons (2 rounded tablespoons) granulated sugar
4 × 15ml spoons (2 rounded tablespoons) currants
25g (1oz) icing sugar
Hot water

1. Prepare a moderately hot oven (200 deg C, 400 deg F, Gas Mark 6). Lightly grease a shallow, 18cm (7in) square tin.
2. Work 75g (3oz) butter on a plate with a round-ended knife, until soft. Shape into an even, flat round; divide in half.
3. Place flour in a bowl. Add the remaining 50g (2oz) butter, cut into small pieces. Rub in with the fingertips until mixture resembles fine breadcrumbs. Add milk and mix to a soft dough. Turn out on to floured board and knead lightly.
4. Roll out to an oblong 30cm by 23cm (12in by 9in). Dot top two-thirds with one half of softened butter. Sprinkle buttered section with 2 × 15ml spoons (1 rounded tablespoon) each of granulated sugar and currants. Fold dough, bringing lower third over centre portion, then fold over top third. Press open edges lightly with a rolling pin, to seal. Half turn dough, so that fold is on right-hand side; roll out dough again to a 30cm by 23cm (12in by 9in) oblong. Spread all over with remaining butter, sugar and currants.

MUFFINS
Makes 14

1 × 5ml spoon (1 level teaspoon) castor sugar
250ml (½ pint) milk
2 × 5ml spoons (2 level teaspoons) dried yeast
450g (1lb) plain flour
2 × 5ml spoons (2 level teaspoons) salt

1. Dissolve sugar in 125ml (¼ pint) hand-hot milk (43 deg C, 110 deg F) from measured milk. Sprinkle dried yeast on top; leave until frothy, about 10 minutes.
2. Place flour and salt in a bowl; mix in yeast liquid and remaining milk with a wooden spoon.
3. Turn out the dough on to a floured board. Knead and stretch dough by folding towards you, then pushing away with the palm of the hand. Give dough a quarter turn and repeat, developing a rocking motion. Knead for about 10 minutes, until dough feels firm and elastic and no longer sticky.
4. Place dough in a bowl. Cover with greased foil or a polythene bag. Leave to rise until dough has doubled and springs back when pressed with a floured finger.
5. Turn out dough on to a floured board and knead lightly. Roll out dough to 6mm (¼in) thickness; cut into rounds, using a 8·5cm (3¼in) cutter. Place on a well-floured baking sheet; dust with flour. Cover with greased foil or polythene; leave to rise until doubled in size.
6. Lightly grease a griddle or large, thick-based frying pan; place over a moderate heat for 2 to 3 minutes.
7. Place muffins, a little apart, on griddle or in pan; cook for 6 minutes. Invert muffins; press down lightly with a fish slice and cook for a further 6 minutes, until golden brown. Remove from griddle or pan and leave to cool on a wire rack. Repeat with remaining muffins.
8. To serve: Split muffins; toast split sides and spread with butter.

Note : Altnernatively, use fresh yeast: Blend 25g (½oz) yeast with 125ml (¼ pint) warm milk (omit sugar) and use at once.

BATH BUNS
Makes 12

Batter

125g (5oz) plain flour

1 × 5ml spoon (1 level teaspoon) castor sugar

2 × 5ml spoons (2 level teaspoons) dried yeast

125ml (¼ pint) hand-hot milk (40 deg C, 110 deg F)

125ml (¼ pint) hand-hot water, less 4 × 15ml spoons (4 tablespoons)

Dough

300g (11oz) plain flour

50g (2oz) margarine

2 eggs

1 × 5ml spoon (1 level teaspoon) salt

75g (3oz) castor sugar

150g (6oz) sultanas

50g (2oz) cut mixed peel

Egg Glaze

1 egg

1 × 5ml spoon (1 level teaspoon)

50g (1½oz) sugar lumps

1. Place batter ingredients in a large bowl. Beat with a wooden spoon until smooth, then leave in a warm place until frothy, about 20 minutes.

2. Place 300g (11oz) flour in a bowl. Add margarine, cut into small pieces, and rub in with the fingertips until mixture resembles fine breadcrumbs. Beat eggs and salt together in a small bowl.

3. Add rubbed-in mixture, eggs, sugar, sultanas and cut mixed peel to batter. Beat well with a wooden spoon or with the hand for about 10 minutes.

4. Cover with greased polythene, or place in a lightly-greased, large saucepan and cover with a lid. Leave to rise for about 1½ hours, or until dough has doubled in size and will spring back when pressed with a floured finger.

5. Lightly grease 2 baking sheets. Beat dough well with a wooden spoon or with the hand for a few minutes. Place tablespoonfuls of the dough on baking sheets. Cover with greased polythene and leave in a warm place for 30 minutes, or until dough has doubled in size.

6. Prepare a hot oven (220 deg C, 425 deg F, Gas Mark 7). Place egg, sugar and 1 tablespoon water in a small bowl. Beat with a fork until well mixed.

7. Place sugar lumps in a paper bag and crush coarsely with a rolling pin.

8. Remove polythene from buns; brush buns with egg glaze and sprinkle with crushed sugar. Bake just above centre of oven for 15 to 20 minutes. Remove from oven; leave to cool on a wire rack.

Note: Alternatively, use 25g (½oz) fresh yeast in place of 2 × 5ml spoons (2 teaspoons) dried yeast; use warm milk and water in place of hand-hot.

Below: *Bath buns*

19

CRUMPETS

Yeast Batter

250ml (½ pint), plus 5×15ml
    spoons (5 tablespoons), hand
    water 40 deg C, (110 deg F)
1×10ml spoon (2 level teaspoons)
    dried yeast
340g (12oz) plain flour
125ml (¼ pint) plus 2×15ml
    spoons (2 tablespoons) milk
1×2·5ml spoon (½ level teaspoon)
    bicarbonate of soda
1×10ml spoon (2 level teaspoons)
    salt

---

1. Measure 5×15ml spoons (5 tablespoons) hand-hot water into a small basin; sprinkle on yeast and leave until frothy, about 10 minutes. Warm mixer bowl and beaters.

2. Place flour, yeast liquid and 250ml (½ pint) hand-hot water in mixer bowl. Run machine at lowest speed, until mixture is smooth and well-blended. Cover with plastic film. Leave until light and frothy, about 30 to 40 minutes.

3. Mix remaining ingredients together; stir into batter (mixture should be fairly liquid).

4. Very lightly grease a griddle or a thick-based frying pan and 4 7·5cm to 9cm (3in to 3½in) rings (egg poaching rings or plain cutters, see note). Place rings on griddle pan and place over a moderate heat for 2 to 3 minutes. (A spot of water should quickly sizzle, when dropped on griddle.) Pour 1 tablespoon batter into each ring; cook gently for about 10 minutes reducing heat slightly when bubbles rise on outer top edges. When surface is set, remove rings and turn crumpets over. Cook for a further 2 to 3 minutes, to brown lightly.

5. Reheat griddle and re-grease if necessary. Grease rings and repeat until all batter is used.

6. To serve: toast lightly on both sides. Serve hot, with butter and honey or jam.

Note : Alternatively, use fresh yeast: Blend 25g (½oz) with 5×15 ml (5 tablespoons) warm water and use at once. If you do not have rings of the size required, cut a piece of foil 28cm by 13cm (11in by 5in). Fold into 4 across the width, to make a strip, 28cm by 3cm (11in by 1¼in). Shape into a circle, 8·5cm (3¼in) in diameter (around a cutter if you have one). Staple ends together.

Below: *Crumpets*

PLAIN SCONES
Makes 8

200g (8oz) self-raising flour
1×2·5ml spoon (½ level teaspoon)
    salt
1×10ml spoons (2 level teaspoons)
    castor sugar
50g (2oz) margarine
7×15ml spoons (7 tablespoons)
    milk

---

1. Prepare a hot oven (230 deg C, 450 deg F, Gas Mark 8). Grease a baking sheet.

2. Place flour, salt and sugar in a bowl. Add margarine, cut into small pieces.

3. Rub in with the fingertips until mixture resembles fine breadcrumbs.

4. Add milk all at once and mix with a fork, to form a soft dough. Turn out on to a floured board and knead lightly with the fingertips.

5. Roll out to 2cm (1in) thickness; using a 6cm (2½in) plain cutter, cut into rounds. Alternatively, roll out to a circle 25cm (1in) thick and cut into 8 wedges. Place on baking sheet, brush with milk and bake, just above centre of oven, until risen and golden brown, for 10 to 12 minutes. Leave to cool on a wire rack.

Variations
Fruit scones: Add 50g (2oz) of

Above: *Plain scones*

Top right: *Fruit scones*

Right: *Cheese scones*

Bottom right: *Orange and cinnamon scones*

cleaned, dried fruit to basic plain scone mixture.

Wholemeal scones: Use 100g (4oz) plain flour, 100g (4oz) wholemeal flour and 2 × 10ml spoons (4 level teaspoons) baking powder instead of 200 g (8oz) self-raising flour in basic plain scone mixture.

Raisin and honey scones: Omit sugar and add 2 × 15ml spoons (2 level tablespoons) honey and 50g (2oz) raisins to basic plain scone mixture.

Orange and cinnamon scones: Add an extra 15ml spoon (1 level tablespoon) castor sugar, then add 1 × 5ml spoon (1 level tablespoon) cinnamon, 50g (2oz) sultanas and grated rind of 1 medium-sized orange to basic plain scone mixture.

Cheese scones: Omit sugar from basic plain scone mixture and add 1 × 2·5ml spoon (½ level teaspoon) dry mustard and 50g (2oz) grated cheese.

Cheese and bacon scones: Add 2 chopped rashers of streaky bacon to cheese scone mixture; brush with milk and sprinkle tops of scones with 25g (1oz) grated cheese before baking.

FRUIT TEA BREAD

400g (1lb) mixed dried fruit
200g (8oz) granulated sugar
250ml (½ pint) warm tea
1 egg
4×15ml spoons (2 rounded tablespoons) thick-cut marmalade
200g (8 oz) plain flour
200g (8 oz) wheatmeal flour
2×10ml spoons (4 level teaspoons) baking powder

1. Place fruit in a bowl. Add sugar and tea; mix together. Leave to soak overnight.

2. Prepare a cool oven (170 deg C, 325 deg F, Gas Mark 3). Grease two ½kg (1lb) loaf tins.

3. Stir egg and marmalade into fruit mixture. Add flours and baking powder; mix well. Divide mixture between tins; level tops with back of spoon.

4. Bake in centre of oven for 1¼ to 1½ hours, until well risen. Test by pressing with the fingers. If cooked, loaves should spring back and have begun to shrink from sides of tins. Leave in tins for 10 minutes, then turn out and leave to cool on a wire rack. Serve sliced and buttered.

Note: The loaves will improve in flavour, if stored for up to 4 weeks in a tin. Alternatively, replace mixed fruit with raisins, and marmalade with pure malt extract.

Below: *Fruit teabread*

Basic Cakes

RICH FRUIT CAKE

Ingredients (Metric)	Round 15cm / Square 12·5cm	Round 18cm / Square 15cm	Round 20·5cm / Square 18cm	Round 23cm / Square 20·5cm	Round 25·5cm / Square 23cm	Round 28cm / Square 25·5cm	Round 30·5cm / Square 28cm	Round 33cm / Square 30·5cm
Currants	225g	300g	400g	525g	625g	750g	900g	1kg 150g
Sultanas	100g	125g	200g	250g	300g	375g	450g	575g
Raisins	100g	125g	200g	250g	300g	375g	450g	575g
Shelled Almonds	25g	25g	50g	75g	75g	75g	125g	125g
Citrus Peel	25g	25g	50g	75g	75g	75g	125g	125g
Glacé Cherries	50g	50g	75g	100g	125g	150g	175g	175g
Plain Flour	125g	150g	200g	250g	325g	375g	450g	550g
Mixed Spice	$\frac{1}{2}$×2·5ml spoon	$\frac{1}{2}$×2·5ml spoon	1×2·5ml spoon	1$\frac{1}{2}$×2·5ml spoon	1$\frac{1}{2}$×2·5ml spoon	1×5ml spoon	1×5ml spoon	1×5ml spoon
Butter or Margarine	125g	150g	200g	250g	325g	375g	450g	550g
Moist Brown Sugar	125g	150g	200g	250g	325g	375g	450g	550g
Lemon (grated rind and juice)	$\frac{1}{2}$	$\frac{1}{2}$	1	1	1$\frac{1}{2}$	1$\frac{1}{2}$	2	2
Eggs (medium-sized)	2	3	3	5	6	7	8	10
Sherry, Rum or Brandy (optional)	1×15ml spoon	5×5ml spoons	3×10ml spoons	4×10ml spoons	3×15ml spoons	4×15ml spoons	4×15ml spoons	6×15ml spoons

Ingredients (Imperial)	Round 6in / Square 5in	Round 7in / Square 6in	Round 8in / Square 7in	Round 9in / Square 8in	Round 10in / Square 9in	Round 11in / Square 10in	Round 12in / Square 11in	Round 13in / Square 12in
Currants	8oz	10oz	14oz	1lb 2oz	1lb 6oz	1lb 10oz	2lb	2lb 8oz
Sultanas	4oz	5oz	7oz	9oz	11oz	13oz	1lb	1lb 4oz
Raisins	4oz	5oz	7oz	9oz	11oz	13oz	1lb	1lb 4oz
Shelled Almonds	1oz	1oz	1$\frac{1}{2}$oz	2$\frac{1}{2}$oz	3oz	3$\frac{1}{2}$oz	4oz	4oz
Citrus Peel	1oz	1oz	1$\frac{1}{2}$oz	2$\frac{1}{2}$oz	3oz	3$\frac{1}{2}$oz	4oz	4oz
Glacé Cherries	1$\frac{1}{2}$oz	1$\frac{1}{2}$oz	3oz	3$\frac{1}{2}$oz	4oz	5oz	6oz	6oz
Plain Flour	4oz	5oz	7oz	9oz	11oz	13oz	1lb	1lb 4oz
Mixed Spice (in level teaspoons)	$\frac{1}{4}$	$\frac{1}{4}$	$\frac{1}{4}$	$\frac{1}{4}$	$\frac{1}{4}$	1	1	1
Butter or Margarine	4oz	5oz	7oz	9oz	11oz	13oz	1lb	1lb 4oz
Moist Brown Sugar	4oz	5oz	7oz	9oz	11oz	13oz	1lb	1lb 4oz
Lemon (grated rind and juice)	$\frac{1}{2}$	$\frac{1}{2}$	1	1	1$\frac{1}{2}$	1$\frac{1}{2}$	2	2
Eggs	2 standard	2 large	3 large	4 large	5 large	6 large	8 standard	10 standard
Sherry, Rum or Brandy, optional (in tablespoons)	1	1$\frac{1}{2}$	2	2$\frac{1}{2}$	3	3$\frac{1}{2}$	4	6

1. Prepare a moderately hot oven (200 deg C, 400 deg F, Gas Mark 6). Line cake tin (see page 24).

2. Prepare ingredients. Fruit: If cleaned fruit is not bought, wash in a colander in a bowl of warm water, and remove any stalks. Spread out to dry thoroughly overnight (if fruit is wet, cake will not keep). Stone raisins, if necessary. Halve cherries, rinse sugar off, peel and chop. Almonds: Boil for one minute, strain and slip off skins. Shred finely. Dry ingredients: Sift flour and spice together. Lemon: Grate rind, avoiding white pith, and squeeze juice. Eggs: Use at room temperature; beat together.

3. Cream butter and sugar together until light and fluffy.

4. Beat in eggs, a little at a time, then add lemon rind, fruit, peel and nuts; mix thoroughly. Stir in flour, spice and lemon juice. Mix well, then place in tin, pressing mixture down sides. Smooth top.

5. Place cake on a double sheet of brown paper on a baking sheet. Reduce oven temperature to cool (170 deg C, 325 deg F, Gas Mark 3) and bake cake in centre of oven, as follows:

1st hour—170 deg C, 325 deg F, Gas Mark 3

2nd hour—150 deg C, 300 deg F, Gas Mark 2

3rd hour—140 deg C, 275 deg F, Gas Mark 1

4th hour—130 deg C, 250 deg F, Gas Mark $\frac{1}{2}$.

If not sufficiently brown after 3 hours' cooking time, cook cake for the 4th hour at 140 deg C, 275 deg F, Gas Mark 1. If cake is sufficiently brown after 3 hours' cooking time, place a sheet of brown paper over top.

6. When cooked, remove from oven and leave to cool in tin. (For cake testing, see below).

7. When quite cold, remove cake from tin and remove paper. To increase keeping time of cake and to ensure moistness, prick cake over top with a skewer and spoon a little sherry, rum or brandy into cake. Invert and treat base similarly. Wrap in foil and store in a tin. Add spirits twice more at weekly intervals.

Lining a Cake Tin

Line with double greaseproof paper. Draw around base of tin, cut out 2 circles; roll tin on a strip of greaseproof paper, marking, from the seam, to exact size of tin, avoiding joins, as these could spoil the shape of cake; cut the strip 5cm (2in) higher than the depth of the cake tin; fold down 2·5cm (1in) along the strip and snip at intervals up to the fold. Brush tin with melted fat and place strip in tin, the folded paper at the bottom. Press paper to sides of tin; fit circles or squares of paper in base; brush again with melted fat, pressing out any bubbles between the paper and tin. Cut a double strip of brown paper or newspaper 2·5cm (1in) higher than depth of tin; place around outside of tin and secure with string.

Cake Testing

To check if a cake is cooked, press with the fingers. If cooked, cake should spring back and have begun to shrink from sides of tin. Leave to cool in tin for 5 minutes. Turn out, remove paper and leave to cool on a wire rack, unless otherwise stated in the recipe.

Below: *Rich fruit cake*

RICH CAKE MIXTURE

1. Prepare oven (see opposite).

2. To prepare baking tins; Brush tartlet tins and ring tin with oil or melted fat. Brush sandwich tins and shallow, square or oblong tins with oil or melted fat; line each base with greaseproof paper; grease paper. Brush deep round tin with melted fat; line base and side with greaseproof paper; grease paper.

3. Cream butter or margarine and sugar together until light and fluffy. Beat egg or eggs together and add gradually, beating after each addition.

4. Fold in flour with a metal spoon to make a soft dropping consistency. Spread mixture evenly in tins and level surface with spoon.

5. Bake in centre of oven (see chart). Cool in tins for 5 to 10 minutes, then turn out, remove paper and leave to cool on a wire rack. *See page 26 for flavourings.*

Quantity (Metric)	Butter or Margarine	Castor Sugar	Eggs	Self-raising Flour	Baking tins	Oven Temperature	Cooking Times
50g	50g	50g	1	50g	1 (18cm) sandwich tin	170 deg C, 325 deg F, Gas Mark 3	20 to 25 minutes
					9 paper baking cases or small tartlet tins	170 deg C, 325 deg F, Gas Mark 3	15 to 20 minutes
					4 (9cm) tartlet tins	170 deg C, 325 deg F, Gas Mark 3	20 to 25 minutes
100g	100g	100g	2	100g	2 (18cm) sandwich tins	170 deg C, 325 deg F, Gas Mark 3	20 to 25 minutes
					1 (20·5cm) sandwich tin or 1 shallow 18cm square tin	170 deg C, 325 deg F, Gas Mark 3	25 to 30 minutes
					18 paper baking cases or small tartlet tins	170 deg C, 325 deg F, Gas Mark 3	15 to 20 minutes
					12 castle pudding or dariole tins	170 deg C, 325 deg F, Gas Mark 3	15 to 20 minutes
150g	150g	150g	3	150g	2 (20·5cm) sandwich tins	170 deg C, 325 deg F, Gas Mark 3	25 to 30 minutes
					1 (28cm by 18cm by 4cm deep) tin	170 deg C, 325 deg F, Gas Mark 3	25 to 30 minutes
					1 deep round (18cm) tin	170 deg C, 325 deg F, Gas Mark 3	1 to $1\frac{1}{4}$ hours
					1 (20·5cm) ring tin	170 deg C, 325 deg F, Gas Mark 3	25 to 30 minutes

Quantity (Imperial)	Butter or Margarine	Castor Sugar	Eggs	Self-raising Flour	Baking Tins	Oven Temperature	Cooking Times
2oz	2oz	2oz	1	2oz	1 (7in) sandwich tin	170 deg C, 325 deg F, Gas Mark 3	25 to 30 minutes
					9 paper baking cases or small tartlet tins	170 deg C, 325 deg F, Gas Mark 3	20 to 25 minutes
					4 ($3\frac{1}{2}$in) tartlet tins	170 deg C, Gas Mark 3	25 to 30 minutes
4oz	4oz	4oz	2	4oz	2 (7in) sandwich tins	170 deg C, 325 deg F, Gas Mark 3	25 to 30 minutes
					1 (8in) sandwich tin or 1 shallow 7in square tin	170 deg C, 325 deg F, Gas Mark 3	30 to 35 minutes
					18 paper baking cases or small tartlet tins	170 deg C, 325 deg F, Gas Mark 3	20 to 25 minutes
					12 castle pudding or dariole tins	170 deg C, 325 deg F, Gas Mark 3	20 to 25 minutes
6oz	6oz	6oz	3	6oz	2 (8in) sandwich tins	170 deg C, 325 deg F, Gas Mark 3	30 to 35 minutes
					1 (11in by 7in by $1\frac{1}{2}$in deep) tin	170 deg C, 325 deg F, Gas Mark 3	30 to 35 minutes
					1 deep round (7in) tin	170 deg C, 325 deg F, Gas Mark 3	$1\frac{1}{4}$ to $1\frac{1}{2}$ hours
					1 (8in) ring tin	170 deg C, 325 deg F, Gas Mark 3	30 to 35 minutes

FLAVOURINGS: Rich Cake Mixture

Quantity	Chocolate	Coffee	Cherry	Coconut	Orange/Lemon
50g	Replace 25g flour with 25g cocoa	Dissolve 1×5ml spoon instant coffee in beaten eggs before adding	Add 25g halved glacé cherries before adding flour	Add 25g desiccated coconut and 1×10ml spoon milk with flour	Add grated rind of 1 small orange or lemon to creamed mixture. Use juice in icing
100g	Replace 25g flour with 25g cocoa	Dissolve 2×5ml spoons instant coffee in beaten eggs before adding	Add 50g halved glacé cherries before adding flour	Add 50g desiccated coconut and 1×15ml spoon milk with flour	Add grated rind of 1 orange or lemon to creamed mixture. Use juice in icing
150g	Replace 50g flour with 50g cocoa	Dissolve 1×15ml spoon instant coffee in beaten eggs before adding	Add 75g halved glacé cherries before adding flour	Add 75g desiccated coconut and 2×15ml spoons milk with flour	Add grated rind of 1 large orange or lemon to creamed mixture. Use juice in icing

Quantity	Chocolate	Coffee	Cherry	Coconut	Orange/Lemon
2oz	Replace ½oz flour with ¼oz cocoa	Dissolve 1 level teaspoon instant coffee in beaten eggs before adding	Add 1oz halved glacé cherries before adding flour	Add 1oz desiccated coconut and 1 dessert-spoon milk with flour	Add grated rind of 1 small orange or lemon to creamed mixture. Use juice in icing
4oz	Replace 1oz flour with 1oz cocoa	Dissolve 1 rounded teaspoon of instant coffee in beaten eggs before adding	Add 2oz halved glacé cherries before adding flour	Add 2oz desiccated coconut and 1 tablespoon milk with flour	Add grated rind of 1 orange or lemon to creamed mixture. Use juice in icing
6oz	Replace 1½oz flour with 1¼oz cocoa	Dissolve 3 level teaspoons instant coffee in beaten eggs before adding	Add 3oz halved glacé cherries before adding flour	Add 3oz desiccated coconut and 3 dessert-spoons milk with flour	Add grated rind of 1 large orange or lemon to creamed mixture. Use juice in icing

SPONGE CAKE OR SWISS ROLL

Quantity (Metric)	Eggs	Castor Sugar	Plain Flour	Baking Powder	Baking Tins	Oven Temperatures	Cooking Times
2 egg	2	50g	50g	1 × 2·5ml spoon	2 (18cm) sandwich tins	180 deg C, 350 deg F, Gas Mark 4	15 to 20 minutes
					1 (20·5cm) sandwich tin or 1 (20·5cm) sponge flan tin	180 deg C, 350 deg F, Gas Mark 4	20 to 25 minutes
					28cm by 18cm Swiss Roll tin	200 deg C, 400 deg F, Gas Mark 6	5 to 8 minutes
					750ml ring jelly mould	180 deg C, 350 deg F, Gas Mark 4	20 to 25 minutes
3 egg	3	75g	75g	1 × 2·5ml spoon	32cm by 22cm Swiss Roll tin	200 deg C, 400 deg F, Gas Mark 6	5 to 8 minutes
					1 litre ring jelly mould	180 deg C, Gas Mark 4	25 to 30 minutes

Quantity (Imperial)	Eggs	Castor Sugar	Plain Flour	Baking Powder	Baking Tins	Oven Temperatures	Cooking Times
2 egg	2	2oz	2oz	½ level teaspoon	2 (7in) sandwich tins	180 deg C, 350 deg F, Gas Mark 4	20 to 25 minutes
					1 (8in) sandwich tin or 1 (8in) sponge flan tin	180 deg C, 350 deg F, Gas Mark 4	25 to 30 minutes
					11in by 7in Swiss Roll tin	200 deg C, 400 deg F, Gas Mark 6	8 to 10 minutes
					1½ pint ring jelly mould	180 deg C, 350 deg F, Gas Mark 4	25 to 30 minutes
3 egg	3	3oz	3oz	½ level teaspoon	12½in by 8½in Swiss Roll tin	200 deg C, 400 deg F, Gas Mark 6	8 to 10 minutes
					2 pint ring jelly mould	180 deg C, 350 deg F, Gas Mark 4	30 to 35 minutes

1. Prepare oven (see above).
2. Prepare baking tins. For sponge cake: Brush sandwich tins with oil or melted fat and line with a circle of greaseproof paper; grease paper. For sponge flan or ring: Brush tins with oil or melted fat. For Swiss roll: Draw around base of Swiss roll tin on greaseproof paper. Cut paper 1·3cm (½in) out from line; crease paper on line. Brush tin with oil or melted fat, press greaseproof paper down into tin, then grease paper.
3. Bring a saucepan of water to boil and remove from heat. Place eggs and sugar in a bowl over saucepan and whisk until mixture becomes thick and leaves a trail when lifted. Remove bowl from saucepan and continue whisking until mixture is cool.
4. Sift flour and baking powder together, then carefully fold into egg mixture with a metal spoon.
5. Pour into prepared tin and shake tin gently to level mixture. Bake in centre of oven (see above).

For sponge cake: Remove from

Left: Sponge cake

FLAVOURINGS

Quantity	Chocolate	Coffee	Orange/Lemon
2 egg	Replace 25g flour with 25g cocoa	Add 1 × 5ml spoon instant coffee to eggs and sugar mixture	Add 1 × 5ml spoon grated rind to eggs and sugar mixture
3 egg	Replace 25g flour with 25g cocoa	Add 2 × 5ml spoons instant coffee to eggs and sugar mixture	Add 2 × 5ml spoons grated rind to eggs and sugar mixture

Quantity	Chocolate	Coffee	Orange/Lemon
2 egg	Replace ½oz flour with ½oz cocoa	Add 1 level teaspoon instant coffee to eggs and sugar mixture	Add 1 level teaspoon grated rind to eggs and sugar mixture
3 egg	Replace ¾oz flour with ¾oz cocoa	Add 1 rounded teaspoon instant coffee to eggs and sugar mixture	Add 1 rounded teaspoon grated rind to eggs and sugar mixture

tin or tins; remove paper. Leave to cool on a wire rack.

6. For Swiss roll: For a jam-filled Swiss roll, while cake is baking, heat 2×15ml spoons (2 tablespoons) of jam in small saucepan. Cut a piece of greaseproof paper about 2.5cm (1in) bigger all round than tin; sprinkle thickly with sugar.

7. Invert cake on to sugared paper. Quickly loosen paper from sides and bottom of cake and carefully remove. Trim edges of cake with a sharp knife. Make a cut halfway through cake 2·5cm (1in) from, and parallel with, the end from which cake will be rolled.

8. Quickly spread cake with warmed jam, if used, taking jam almost to cut edges.

9. To make a firm start to the roll, press half-cut edge down and hold with one hand; using the paper, roll cake firmly. Hold cake for a moment, with greaseproof paper around, to set cake. Remove paper and leave Swiss roll to cool on a wire rack.

Note: For a butter-icing or cream-filled Swiss roll: Omit jam and roll cake, with greaseproof paper inside. When cool, unroll, remove paper, and fill with flavoured butter icing (see recipe on page 30) or cream.

Below: *Swiss roll*

The Art of Icing

ALMOND PASTE

Mix all dry ingredients together. Stir in sufficient egg yolk, almond essence and lemon juice to bind to a stiff paste. (Store egg whites in a cool place in covered jar for use in royal icing.)

Ingredients (Metric)	Round 15cm / Square 12·5cm	Round 18cm / Square 15cm	Round 20·5cm / Square 18cm	Round 23cm / Square 20·5cm	Round 25·5cm / Square 23cm	Round 28cm / Square 25·5cm	Round 30·5cm / Square 28cm	Round 33cm / Square 30·5cm
Ground Almonds	200g	250g	300g	450g	600g	700g	850g	1kg
Icing Sugar	100g	125g	150g	225g	300g	350g	425g	½kg
Castor Sugar	100g	125g	150g	225g	300g	350g	425g	½kg
Sufficient egg yolk to bind (save whites for Royal icing)								
Almond Essence	1×2·5ml spoon	1×2·5ml spoon	1×2·5ml spoon	1×2·5ml spoon	1×5ml spoon	1×5ml spoon	1×5ml spoon	1×5ml spoon
Lemon Juice	1×5ml spoon	1×5ml spoon	1×5ml spoon	1×5ml spoon	1×10ml spoon	1×10ml spoon	1×10ml spoon	1×10ml spoon

Ingredients (Imperial)	Round 6in / Square 5in	Round 7in / Square 6in	Round 8in / Square 7in	Round 9in / Square 8in	Round 10in / Square 9in	Round 11in / Square 10in	Round 12in / Square 11in	Square 12in
Ground Almonds	8oz	10oz	12oz	1lb	1lb 4oz	1lb 8oz	1lb 12oz	2lb
Icing Sugar	4oz	5oz	6oz	8oz	10oz	12oz	14oz	1lb
Castor Sugar	4oz	5oz	6oz	8oz	10oz	12oz	14oz	1lb
Sufficient egg yolk to bind (save whites for Royal icing)								
Almond Essence	½ teaspoon	½ teaspoon	½ teaspoon	½ teaspoon	1 teaspoon	1 teaspoon	1 teaspoon	1 teaspoon
Lemon Juice	1 teaspoon	1 teaspoon	1 teaspoon	1 teaspoon	2 teaspoons	2 teaspoons	2 teaspoons	2 teaspoons

ROYAL ICING

Ingredients (Metric)	Round 15cm / Square 12·5cm	Round 18cm / Square 15cm	Round 20·5cm / Square 18cm	Round 23cm / Square 20·5cm	Round 25·5cm / Square 23cm	Round 28cm / Square 25·5cm	Round 30·5cm / Square 28cm	Round 33cm / Square 30·5cm
Icing Sugar	450g	600g	¾kg	¾kg	1kg	1kg	1kg 200g	1kg 200g
Egg Whites	2 to 3	3	4	4	5 to 6	5 to 6	6 to 7	6 to 7
Glycerine or clear honey (optional, but omit for a tiered cake)	1×5ml spoon	1×5ml spoon	1½×5ml spoon	1½×5ml spoon	1×10ml spoon	1×10ml spoon	2½×5ml spoons	2½×5ml spoons

Ingredients (Imperial)	Round 6in / Square 5in	Round 7in / Square 6in	Round 8in / Square 7in	Round 9in / Square 8in	Round 10in / Square 9in	Round 11in / Square 10in	Round 12in / Square 11in	Square 12in
Icing Sugar	1lb	1¼lb	1½lb	1½lb	2lb	2lb	2lb 8oz	2lb 8oz
Egg Whites	2 to 3	3	4	4	5 to 6	5 to 6	6	6
Glycerine or clear honey (optional but omit for a tiered cake)	1 teaspoon	1 teaspoon	1½ teaspoons	1½ teaspoons	2 teaspoons	2 teaspoons	2½ teaspoons	2½ teaspoons

1. Sieve icing sugar.
2. Put egg whites in a clean, grease-free bowl. Add sufficient icing sugar and mix to a consistency similar to thick cream.
3. Beat with wooden spoon for 10 to 15 minutes, until icing is very stiff and stands up in stiff peaks when spoon is lifted out of bowl. Alternatively, beat with an electric mixer on slowest speed until stiff.
4. Beat in honey or glycerine, if used. Cover bowl with a damp cloth during the whole time it is being used, to prevent a skin forming. To store, place icing in an airtight plastic container and close lid securely.

ITALIAN ICING

75g (3oz) icing sugar
1 egg white
Food colouring

1. Place icing sugar and egg white in a bowl over a saucepan of hot water.
2. Whisk mixture until thick. Add a few drops of food colouring and continue whisking until mixture is stiff and standing in peaks. Remove bowl from saucepan and whisk for 1 minute.
3. Place icing in a greaseproof paper piping bag fitted with a small star tube. Pipe 'stars' on grease-proof or waxed paper. Leave in a cool, dry place to harden. Use to decorate cakes.

RICH BUTTERCREAM

50g (2oz) granulated sugar
1 egg yolk
125g (5oz) unsalted butter

1. Place 6 × 15ml spoons (6 tablespoons) water and the sugar in a small saucepan and heat slowly until dissolved. Increase heat and boil until syrup forms a thread between 2 teaspoons or until syrup registers 104 deg C (20 deg F), on a sugar thermometer.
2. Whisk egg yolk in a small basin, gradually whisk in sugar syrup and continue to whisk until cold.
3. Cut butter into small pieces and whisk into egg mixture, whisking well after each addition.

AMERICAN FROSTING

4 × 15ml spoons (2½ fluid oz) water
200g (8oz) granulated sugar
1 egg white
Food colouring (optional)

1. Place water in a thick saucepan, with granulated sugar, and heat slowly until dissolved. Boil until syrup forms a soft ball when dropped in a saucer of cold water, or syrup registers 115 deg C (240 deg F) on a sugar thermometer.
2. Meanwhile, place egg white in a clean, grease-free bowl and whisk until stiff and dry. Pour on the sugar syrup slowly, and continue whisking until mixture thickens. Add a few drops of colouring, if desired, and continue whisking until mixture will form soft peaks.
3. Place cake on a plate or cake board, quickly spread frosting over top and side of cake and make peaks with a round-ended knife. Leave to set.

GLACE ICING

250g (10oz) icing sugar
3 × 15ml spoons (3 tablespoons) hot water, lemon or orange juice, or black coffee
Food colouring (optional)

1. Sieve icing sugar into a basin. Add liquid until icing thickly coats back of spoon.
2. Add a few drops of food colouring, if desired. Use icing to coat top and side of a 20·5cm (8in) sandwich cake.

BUTTER ICING

1. Sieve icing sugar into a bowl. Add butter and beat together until light and fluffy.
2. Add a little warm water or flavouring and beat until smooth. Use to fill or ice a cake.
See chart opposite for ingredients.

Butter	Icing Sugar	Vanilla	Lemon/Orange	Chocolate	Coffee
25g	50g	1 drop essence and a little warm water	1×2·5ml spoon grated rind and 1×10ml spoon juice	1×2·5ml spoon cocoa dissolved in 1×5ml spoon boiling water, then cooled	1×2·5ml spoon instant coffee dissolved in 1×5ml spoon boiling water, then cooled
50g	100g	2 drops essence and a little warm water	1×5ml spoon grated rind and 1×15ml spoon juice	1×5ml spoon cocoa dissolved in 1×10ml spoon boiling water, then cooled	1×5ml spoon instant coffee dissolved in 1×10ml spoon boiling water, then cooled
75g	150g	3 drops essence and a little warm water	1½×5ml spoon grated rind and 1×15ml spoon juice	1½×5ml spoons cocoa dissolved in 1×15ml spoon boiling water, then cooled	1½×5ml spoons instant coffee dissolved in 1×15ml spoon boiling water, then cooled
100g	200g	4 drops essence and a little warm water	1×10ml spoon grated rind and 1 to 2×15ml spoons juice	1×10ml spoon cocoa dissolved in 2×10ml spoons boiling water, then cooled	1×10ml spoon instant coffee dissolved in 2×10ml spoons boiling water, then cooled
125g	250g	1×2·5ml spoon essence and a little warm water	Grated rind and 2×15ml spoons juice	1×15ml spoon cocoa dissolved in 2×15ml spoons boiling water, then cooled	1×15ml spoon instant coffee dissolved in 2×15ml spoons boiling water, then cooled
150g	300g	1×2·5ml spoon essence and a little warm water	Grated rind and 2×15ml spoons juice	2×10ml spoons cocoa dissolved in 2×15ml spoons boiling water, then cooled	2×10ml spoons instant coffee dissolved in 2×15ml spoons boiling water, then cooled

Butter	Icing Sugar	Vanilla	Lemon/Orange	Chocolate	Coffee
1oz	2oz	1 drop essence and a little warm water	¼ level teaspoon grated rind and 2 teaspoons juice	½ level teaspoon cocoa dissolved in 1 teaspoon boiling water, then cooled	½ level teaspoon instant coffee dissolved in 1 teaspoon boiling water, then cooled
2oz	4oz	2 drops essence and a little warm water	1 level teaspoon grated rind and 3 teaspoons juice	1 level teaspoon cocoa dissolved in 2 teaspoons boiling water, then cooled	1 level teaspoon instant coffee dissolved in 2 teaspoons boiling water, then cooled
3oz	6oz	3 drops essence and a little warm water	1½ level teaspoons grated rind and 1 tablespoon juice	1½ level teaspoons cocoa dissolved in 1 tablespoon boiling water, then cooled	1½ level teaspoons instant coffee dissolved in 3 teaspoons boiling water, then cooled
4oz	8oz	4 drops essence and a little warm water	2 level teaspoons grated rind and 1 to 2 tablespoons juice	2 level teaspoons cocoa dissolved in 4 teaspoons boiling water, then cooled	2 level teaspoons instant coffee dissolved in 4 teaspoons boiling water, then cooled
5oz	10oz	½ teaspoon essence and a little warm water	Grated rind and 2 tablespoons juice	3 level teaspoons cocoa dissolved in 6 teaspoons boiling water, then cooled	3 level teaspoons instant coffee dissolved in 6 teaspoons boiling water, then cooled
6oz	12oz	½ teaspoon essence and a little warm water	Grated rind and 2 to 3 tablespoons juice	1 level tablespoon cocoa dissolved in 2 tablespoons boiling water, then cooled	1 level tablespoon instant coffee dissolved in 2 tablespoons boiling water, then cooled

Piped Cake Designs

A cake decorated with piping has a smart, professional look. Piping is simple to do, and is ideal for decorating cakes with fresh cream, butter icing and royal icing. Practise a little of the design on an upturned plate before piping on the cake itself.

Paper piping bags are the best containers to use when decorating cakes with royal icing or butter icing. Use good-quality grease-proof paper, non-stick household vegetable parchment, or waxed paper.

To make 4 Piping Bags: Cut a piece of paper, 38cm by 25·3cm (15in by 10in), in half, across the width (diagram 1). *See overleaf for illustration.*

Fold one half over so that the 2 points at top are at right angles (diagram 2). Using a sharp knife, slit along fold to make 2 triangular pieces, each with a blunt corner. Mark corners **A, B, C** (see diagram) with pencil. Hold paper with the thumb of the left hand on the long edge below corner **(C)**. With the right hand, fold blunt corner **(A)** into position just below corner **(C)**, forming a cone (see diagram 3). Bring corner **(B)** across the cone to the outside of piping bag (diagram 4) until it fits exactly behind corner (diagram 5). The point of the cone should be sharp; if it is open, move corners **(A)** and **(B)** up and down until point is sharp. Fold corners over twice to hold piping bag firmly together (diagrams 6 and 7). Repeat with remaining pieces of paper.

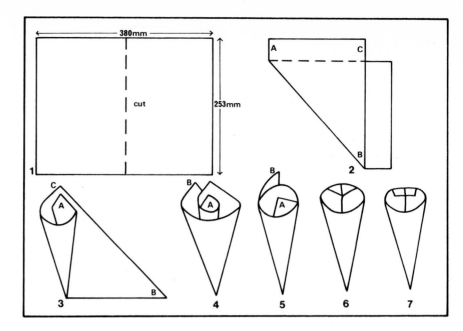

Piping tubes: Small metal piping tubes, without screw ends, used with greasproof paper piping bags, are easiest to use for fine work in butter and royal icing.

Piping tubes are available both plain (or writing) and star. Two of each type would be sufficient for most purposes: Nos 2 and 4 plain tubes and Nos 6 and 9 star tubes. Tubes are also available for making shapes and leaves.

Large piping tubes, sometimes called Savoy tubes, are used with nylon piping bags. They are available in both plain and star designs, and are used for piping fresh cream, rich butter cream, meringues and some biscuit mixtures (and even potato for savoury dishes).

To Fit a Piping Tube: For a plain tube, cut piping bag about 6mm ($\frac{1}{4}$in) from end of point and drop in tube. The tube should extend one-third of its length. For a star tube, cut between 6mm and 1·3cm ($\frac{1}{4}$in and $\frac{1}{2}$in) from point.

To Fill Piping Bag: Hold piping bag with fold between thumb and first finger of one hand. Using a round-ended knife, half fill with the icing (do not overfill), pressing icing down into the bag against the thumb. Fold over top of bag, bring corners to centre and fold over again.

To use Piping Bag: Hold bag between first and second fingers of right hand. Press out icing with thumb on top of bag. Use left hand under right wrist as an additional support when piping.

Piping with Butter Icing: Butter icing must be fairly soft for piping star and shell designs. Beat in a little hot water to mix it to the required consistency, if necessary. Aim at good, rounded-shaped stars, with points where the tube is lifted off. Writing in butter icing is difficult; a No 4 tube must be used with soft butter icing.

Piping with Cream: Use a large star or plain tube in a nylon piping bag. Cream must be whipped until it just holds its shape. Avoid overwhipping, or the cream may curdle when it is piped out. It is best to use a mixture of double and single creams.

Piping with Royal Icing: Royal icing for piping must be stiffer than that used for covering cakes. Add a little sieved icing sugar until the icing stands in stiff peaks. Stiffer icing is required for star tubes than for plain tubes. Keep icing bowl covered; cover full piping bags with damp cloth when not in use.

Straight Lines: Use a plain tube. Place tube at starting point, then lift up and squeeze icing out of bag with thumb. Bring down at end of marked line. Used to decorate tops of cakes. Curved lines, scallops and writing can be done in the same way.

Trellis: Use a fine, plain tube. Pipe parallel straight lines of icing. Leave to dry for about 30 minutes, then repeat parallel lines of icing in the opposite directions. This can be repeated for a third and fourth layer in the same position as the first and second.

Stars: Hold star tube upright and flat on surface, press out icing to form a star, then pull off sharply. Also used for piping butter icing and cream.

Shells: Hold star tube at an angle of 45 deg to starting point. Press out icing, lift tube, then bring down towards you and pull away to a 'tail'. Repeat, starting on tail of previous shell; continue in a row, developing a rocking movement. Also used for piping butter icing and cream.

Scribbling: Use a fine plain tube. Hold the tube upright and flat on surface, press out icing, moving tube continuously, in small circular movements.

Small whirls: Hold star tube upright and flat on surface. Press out icing in a small, circular, clockwise movement, finishing in a star, then pull off sharply. Also used for piping butter icing and cream.

Favourite Cakes

MOIST GINGERBREAD

4×15ml spoons (4 level tablespoons) golden syrup

4×15ml spoons (4 level tablespoons) treacle

7×15ml spoons (7 tablespoons) oil

100g (4oz) soft brown sugar (light)

125ml ($\frac{1}{4}$ pint) milk

200g (8oz) plain flour

1×2·5ml spoon ($\frac{1}{2}$ level teaspoon) bicarbonate of soda

1×2·5ml spoon ($\frac{1}{2}$ level teaspoon) salt

3×15ml spoons (3 level teaspoons) ground ginger

1 egg

1. Prepare a cool oven (150 deg C, 300 deg F, Gas Mark 2). Brush a deep, 18cm (7in) square cake tin with melted fat. Line base of tin with greaseproof paper; grease paper.

2. Measure golden syrup and treacle carefully, levelling off spoon with a knife and making sure there is none on underside of spoon. Place in a medium-sized saucepan, with oil, brown sugar and milk.

3. Heat gently for about 5 minutes until sugar has dissolved; remove from heat and leave to cool.

4. Sift flour, bicarbonate of soda, salt and ginger into a bowl. Make a 'well' in centre of flour; add melted ingredients and egg. Mix together with a wooden spoon; beat for 1 to 2 minutes until smooth.

5. Pour mixture into tin; bake in centre of oven for 50 minutes to 1 hour 15 minutes. Leave to cool in tin for 15 minutes. Loosen edges with a round-ended knife, turn out gingerbread and remove paper; leave to cool completely on a wire rack.

Note: Gingerbread improves with keeping. Store in a tin for up to one week.

Below: *Moist gingerbread*

DUNDEE CAKE

50g (2oz) whole almonds
150g (6oz) butter or margarine
150g (6oz) soft brown sugar
150g (6oz) sultanas
150g (6oz) currants
150g (6oz) seedless raisins
25g (1oz) cut mixed peel
150g (6oz) plain flour
1×2·5ml spoon (½ level teaspoon) baking powder
1×10ml spoon (1 rounded teaspoon) mixed spice
3 eggs

1. Place almonds in a small saucepan, cover with water and bring to boil. Drain, and remove skins.
2. Prepare a cool oven (150 deg C, 300 deg F, Gas Mark 2). Brush a deep, round 17·5cm (7in) cake tin with melted fat or oil. Line base and side with greaseproof paper; grease paper.
3. Place all ingredients in a bowl, except for whole almonds, and mix together with a wooden spoon; beat for 2 to 3 minutes (or 1 to 2 minutes if using a hand mixer) until mixture is smooth and glossy.
4. Place mixture in tin; level top with back of a wet metal spoon. Arrange almonds in rings on top of cake and gently press into cake mixture.
5. Bake in centre of oven for 3 to 3½ hours. Test by pressing with the fingers. If cooked, cake should spring back and have begun to shrink from side of tin. Remove from oven and leave to cool in tin for 30 minutes. Turn out, remove the paper and leave the cake to cool completely on a wire rack.

Right: Dundee cake

CIDER CRUMBLE CAKE

450g (1lb) self-raising flour
1×5ml spoon (1 level teaspoon) salt
100g (4oz) soft brown sugar (dark)
3×15ml spoons (3 level tablespoons) black treacle
2 eggs
6×15ml spoons (6 tablespoons) oil
250ml (½ pint) sweet cider

Crumble Topping

50g (1½oz) shelled walnuts
50g (1½oz) butter
50g (1½oz) self-raising flour
1×2·5ml spoon (½ level teaspoon) ground cinamon
50g (2oz) demerara sugar
3×15ml spoons (3 level tablespoons) thick-cut marmalade

1. Prepare a moderate oven (180 deg C, 350 deg F, Gas Mark 4). Brush a deep 23cm (9in) round, loose-bottomed cake tin with melted fat. Line base and side with greaseproof paper; grease paper.
2. Place flour, salt and soft brown sugar into a bowl. Measure treacle carefully, levelling off spoon with the back of a knife and making sure there is none on underside of spoon; place in a basin; add eggs and oil and beat with a fork.
3. Stir in cider gradually, beating well after each addition. Make a well in centre of flour; add treacle mixture. Mix together with a wooden spoon; beat until smooth.
4. Pour mixture into prepared tin; level top with the back of a metal spoon. Bake in centre of oven for 45 minutes.
5. Meanwhile, coarsely chop walnuts. Place butter, flour and cinnamon in a medium-sized bowl. Rub in with the fingertips until mixture resembles fine breadcrumbs. Add walnuts and 25g (1oz) demerara sugar. Mix together.
6. Remove cake from oven, quickly spread surface of cake with marmalade and sprinkle with topping and remaining 25g (1oz) demerara sugar. Return to oven for a further 25 minutes.
7. Remove from oven. Leave to cool in tin for 10 minutes. Carefully turn out; remove paper and leave to cool on a wire rack. Store in a tin.

Note: This improves in flavour if kept for 2 to 3 days.

HONEY AND SPICE CAKE

Topping

25g (1oz) butter
3×15ml spoons (3 level tablespoons) clear honey
50g (2oz) Rice Krispies

Cake

250g (10oz) self-raising flour
1×5ml spoon (1 level teaspoon) baking powder
1×5ml spoon (1 level teaspoon) mixed spice
1×2·5ml spoon (½ level teaspoon) ground cinamon
200g (8oz) soft margarine
150g (6oz) castor sugar
3 eggs
3×15ml spoons (3 level tablespoons) clear honey

1. Prepare a cool oven (170 deg C, (325 deg F, Gas Mark 3). Brush a deep 20·5cm (8in) round cake tin with melted fat. Line base and side with greaseproof paper; grease paper.
2. To make topping: place butter in a small saucepan. Measure honey carefully, levelling off spoon with the back of a knife and making

COUNTRY FRUIT CAKE

300g (12oz) plain flour
3 × 5ml spoons (3 level teaspoons)
  baking powder
150g (6oz) margarine
150g (6oz) soft brown sugar
  (light)
150g (6oz) sultanas
150g (6oz) currants
2 × 15ml spoons (2 level
  tablespoons) golden syrup
3 eggs
2 × 15ml spoons (1 rounded
  tablespoon) marmalade
4 × 15ml spoons (2 rounded
  tablespoons) brown sugar

---

1. Prepare a cool oven (150 deg C, 300 deg F, Gas Mark 2). Brush a deep, square 20·5cm (8in) tin with melted fat and line base and sides with greaseproof paper; grease paper.
2. Sift flour and baking powder into a bowl. Add margarine, cut into small pieces, and rub in with the fingertips until mixture resembles fine breadcrumbs. Stir in soft brown sugar and dried fruits.
3. Measure golden syrup carefully, levelling off spoon with a knife and making sure there is none on underside of spoon. Place in a basin and add eggs and marmalade; beat well. Stir into dry ingredients and mix well.
4. Place mixture in tin; level top with back of spoon. Sprinkle top with brown sugar. Bake in centre of oven for 2 to 2½ hours. Test by pressing with the fingers. If cooked, cake should spring back and have begun to shrink from sides of tin.
5. Leave to cool in tin for 30 minutes; turn out, remove paper and leave to cool completely on a wire rack.

Note: Country Fruit Cake stores for up to 2 weeks in a tin.

---

sure there is none on underside of spoon. Add to butter and place over a moderate heat until butter has melted. Remove from heat, allow to cool slightly and stir in Rice Krispies.
3. Sift flour, baking powder, mixed spice and cinnamon into a bowl; add remaining cake ingredients and mix together with a wooden spoon. Beat for 2 to 3 minutes until mixture is smooth and glossy.
4. Place mixture in tin; level top with back of spoon. Sprinkle topping over cake. Bake in centre of oven for about 1¼ to 2 hours. Test by pressing with the fingers. If cooked, the cake should spring back and have begun to shrink from side of tin.
5. Leave cake to cool in tin for 10 minutes, then turn out, remove paper, and leave to cool completely on a wire rack. Store in a tin.

YOGHOURT AND DATE CAKE

100g (4oz) butter
50g (2oz) soft brown sugar (dark)
1 × 15ml spoon (1 tablespoon)
  treacle
3 × 15ml spoons (3 level
  tablespoons) golden syrup
75g (3oz) stoned dates
75g (3oz) shelled almonds
1 150ml (5·3 fluid oz) carton
  natural yoghourt
2 eggs
200g (8oz) plain flour
1 × 5ml spoon (1 level teaspoon)
  mixed spice
1 × 2·5ml spoon (½ level teaspoon)
  bicarbonate of soda
Icing sugar

---

1. Prepare a cool oven (150 deg C, 300 deg F, Gas Mark 2). Brush a 1 litre (2 pint) plain ring mould with melted fat.
2. Place butter and brown sugar in a small saucepan. Measure treacle and golden syrup carefully, levelling off spoon with a knife and making sure there is none on underside of spoon; add to saucepan. Stir over a moderate heat until butter has melted. Remove from heat and allow to cool.
3. Coarsely chop dates and almonds. Beat yoghourt and eggs together. Sift flour, spice and bicarbonate of soda into a bowl. Add dates, almonds, melted mixture and yoghourt mixture; mix well with a wooden spoon.
4. Pour mixture into prepared mould and bake in centre of oven for 60 to 70 minutes. Test by pressing with the fingers. If cooked, cake should spring back and have begun to shrink from sides of mould.
5. Allow to cool in mould for 10 minutes. Invert on to a wire rack, remove mould and leave to cool. Dust with icing sugar before serving.

Note: Yoghourt and Date Cake improves in flavour if kept for 2 to 3 days in a tin.

CARAMEL BROWNIE CAKE

150g (6oz) plain chocolate
2×15ml spoons (2 tablespoons) boiling water
100g (4oz) butter
100g (4oz) castor sugar
1×5ml spoon (1 teaspoon) vanilla essence
2 eggs
50g (2oz) shelled walnuts
100g (4oz) self-raising flour
½×2·5ml spoon (¼ level teaspoon) salt

Caramel Topping
100g (4oz) granulated sugar

1. Prepare a moderate oven (190 deg C, 375 deg F, Gas Mark 5). Brush an 20·5cm (8in) round cake tin with melted fat. Line base with greaseproof paper, grease paper.
2. Break up chocolate; place in a basin with water and butter. Place basin over a saucepan of hot, but not boiling, water; stir occasionally until chocolate and butter have melted. Remove basin from saucepan.
3. Add castor sugar and vanilla essence to chocolate mixture, mix well and allow to cool slightly.

Left, clockwise from top: Country fruit cake, yoghourt and date cake, cider crumble cake, honey and spice cake, caramel brownie cake

Beat eggs together in a small bowl; coarsely chop walnuts.
4. Sift flour and salt together into a bowl; make a 'well' in centre of flour. Add chocolate mixture, eggs and walnuts; beat together until mixture is smooth and glossy.
5. Pour into prepared tin. Bake in centre of oven for 45 minutes to 1 hour. Test by pressing with the fingers. If cooked, cake should spring back and have begun to shrink from side of tin.
6. Leave to cool in tin for 5 minutes; turn out and leave to cool completely on a wire rack. Cut a strip of foil 23cm (9in) long by 7·5cm (3in) wide. Turn cake upside-down and wrap foil around cake so that there is approximately a 2cm (¾in) rim of foil above edge of cake.
7. Place granulated sugar and 4×15ml spoons (4 tablespoons) water in a heavy quality saucepan; heat slowly, stirring occasionally, until sugar has dissolved. Increase heat; boil syrup without stirring until syrup has turned a deep golden brown. Remove from heat, allow bubbles to subside and quickly pour over cake.
8. When topping is almost set, lightly mark into 16 wedges with an oiled knife. Remove foil when topping is set.

Note: Store Caramel Brownie Cake for up to 1 week in a tin.

CHOCOLATE AND ORANGE SLICE

Filling
1 medium-sized orange
50g (1½oz) butter or margarine
250g (10oz) icing sugar

Cake
6×15ml spoons (6 level tablespoons) golden syrup
6×15ml spoons (6 level tablespoons) cocoa
100g (4oz) margarine
200g (8oz) plain biscuits

1. Scrub orange; cut in half. Cut a thin slice from each orange half; reserve for decoration.
2. Squeeze juice from both orange halves; grate rind from shells.
3. Place 2 tablespoons orange juice, rind and 50g (1½oz) butter or margarine in a medium-sized saucepan. Heat gently until butter or margarine has melted; remove from heat.
4. Sieve icing sugar; stir into orange juice mixture and beat with a wooden spoon until smooth. Leave until cold.
5. Line base and sides of a 450g (1lb) loaf tin with foil, overlapping rim of tin by 5cm (2in).
6. Measure golden syrup care-

fully, levelling off spoon with a knife and making sure there is none on underside of spoon. Place in a medium-sized saucepan with cocoa and 100g (4oz) margarine. Heat gently until margarine has melted, stirring occasionally. Remove from heat.

7. Place biscuits between 2 sheets of greaseproof paper, crush lightly with a rolling pin.

8. Stir biscuits into chocolate mixture until evenly coated.

9. Press one-third of biscuit mixture well down in tin, levelling top with back of a metal spoon. Spread half the filling over biscuit layer. Repeat with another one-third of biscuits and remaining filling. Top with remaining biscuits, pressing well down and levelling top. Bring foil over top of tin, to cover surface of biscuits; place in refrigerator and leave for at least 2 hours or overnight.

10. Open foil; invert cake on to a serving dish. Remove foil carefully.

11. Cut each reserved orange slice into 4; arrange quarters, overlapping, on top of cake.

MADEIRA CAKE

150g (6oz) soft margarine
150g (6oz) castor sugar
200g (8oz) plain flour
3 × 2·5ml spoons (1½ level
   teaspoons) baking powder
3 eggs
2 thin strips candied citrus peel

1. Prepare a cool oven (170 deg C, 325 deg F, Gas Mark 3).

2. Brush a deep 18cm (7in) round cake tin with melted fat. Line base and side with greaseproof paper; grease paper.

3. Place margarine, sugar, flour, baking powder and eggs in a bowl. Mix together with a wooden spoon and heat for 1 to 2 minutes, until mixture is well blended.

4. Place mixture in tin; level top. Arrange peel in centre.

5. Bake in centre of oven for 1¼ to 1½ hours. Leave to cool in tin for 5 to 10 minutes. Turn out, remove paper and leave to cool completely on a wire rack.

NUT AND CHERRY-TOPPED SHORTBREAD
Makes 8 wedges

Shortbread
150g (6oz) plain flour
50g (2oz) castor sugar
100g (4oz) margarine

Topping
75g (3oz) glacé cherries
50g (2oz) hazelnuts
3 × 15ml spoons (3 level
   tablespoons) thick honey

1. Prepare a cool oven (170 deg C, 325 deg F, Gas Mark 3).

2. Place a 20·5cm (8in) plain flan ring on a baking sheet (or use a 20·5cm (8in) sandwich tin). Brush flan ring and baking sheet or tin with melted fat or oil.

3. Place flour and sugar in a bowl; add margarine, cut into small pieces, and rub in with the fingertips until mixture begins to stick.

4. Place mixture in flan ring or tin; level top with back of a metal spoon. Press down lightly.

5. Bake in centre of oven for 30 to 35 minutes, until shortbread is lightly browned at edges.

6. Leave to cool on baking sheet or tin; remove when cold.

7. To make topping: Cut cherries into quarters; chop nuts finely.

8. Measure honey carefully, levelling off spoon with a knife and making sure there is none on underside of spoon. Place in a small saucepan and bring to boil; stir in cherries and nuts. Pour topping over shortbread; spread evenly, to cover top.

9. When topping has set, cut shortbread into 8 wedges.

Right, clockwise from top: *Madeira cake, nut and cherry-topped shortbread, chocolate and orange slice*

CORN OIL CAKE

125g (5oz) self-raising flour
1 × 5ml spoon (1 level teaspoon)
   baking powder
½ × 2·5ml spoon (¼ level teaspoon)
   salt
100g (4oz) castor sugar
7 × 15ml spoons (7 tablespoons)
   corn oil
2 × 15ml spoons (2 tablespoons)
   milk
2 eggs
½ × 2·5ml spoon (¼ teaspoon)
   vanilla essence
Raspberry jam
Granulated sugar

1. Prepare a moderate oven (180 deg C, 350 deg F, Gas Mark 4).
2. Brush 2 18cm (7in) sandwich tins with oil and line bases with circles of greaseproof paper; grease paper.
3. Sift flour, baking powder and salt together into a bowl; add castor sugar.

4. Measure oil into a basin; add milk, eggs and vanilla essence, then whisk together. Add to dry ingredients and mix well. Beat for 1 minute, until mixture is smooth and creamy.
5. Divide mixture equally between tins. (Check by weight: Either counter-balance filled tins on balance scales or weigh separately on spring-balance scales.) Cook in centre of oven for 20 to 25 minutes, until well risen and golden brown. Test by pressing with the fingers. If cooked, cakes should spring back and have begun to shrink from sides of tins.
6. Loosen cakes from sides of tins and turn out. Remove paper and leave to cool on a wire rack.
7. When cold, sandwich cakes together with raspberry jam and sprinkle top with granulated sugar.

Below: *Corn oil cake*

RASPBERRY CREAM CAKE
For 8 portions

2 eggs
Castor sugar
50g (2oz) plain flour
1 × 2·5ml (½ level teaspoon)
   baking powder
¼kg (½lb) fresh or frozen
   raspberries, just thawed
Icing sugar
170ml (6 fluid oz) carton double
   cream

1. Prepare a moderate oven (180 deg C, 350 deg F, Gas Mark 4). Brush a 20·5cm (8in) sandwich tin with melted fat and line base with greaseproof paper; grease paper.
2. Bring a saucepan of water to boil; remove from heat. Place eggs and 50g (2oz) castor sugar in a bowl over saucepan; whisk until mixture becomes thick and leaves a trail when whisk is lifted. Remove bowl from saucepan; whisk until mixture is cool.
3. Sift flour and baking powder

Above: *Raspberry cream cake*

together; carefully fold into the egg mixture with a metal spoon.

4. Pour into prepared tin; shake tin gently, to level mixture. Bake in centre of oven for 20 to 30 minutes. Test by pressing with the fingers. If cooked, cake should spring back and have begun to shrink from side of tin. Remove from tin; remove paper. Leave cake to cool on a wire rack.

5. Reserve 13 raspberries for decoration; place rest in a basin, with 1 to 2 × 15ml spoons (1 to 2 tablespoons) castor sugar. Stir lightly; leave for 15 minutes.

6. Cut cake in half horizontally. Cut top into 8 wedges and dredge with icing sugar. Whisk cream until thick. Spoon syrup from raspberries over cake base. Lightly fold fruit into cream and spread mixture over base. Arrange sponge wedges on top of cream, slightly overlapping. Place 5 raspberries in centre and remaining raspberries around edge of cake.

BARBADOS SWIRL CAKE

Cake
150g (6oz) margarine
150g (6oz) castor sugar
3 eggs
175g (7oz) self-raising flour
1 × 15ml spoon (1 tablespoon) milk
1 × 5ml spoon (1 level teaspoon) mixed spice
1 × 5ml spoon (1 level teaspoon) ground cinnamon
1 × 5ml spoon (1 level teaspoon) ground nutmeg
1 × 15ml spoon (1 level tablespoon) custard powder
1 × 15ml spoon (1 level tablespoon) treacle

Frosting
300g (12oz) icing sugar
100g (4oz) butter
100g (4oz) soft brown sugar (dark)
3 × 15ml spoons (3 tablespoons) milk
1 × 5ml spoon (1 teaspoon) vanilla essence

1. Prepare a cool oven (170 deg C, 325 deg F, Gas Mark 3). Brush a 16·5cm (6½in) round cake tin with melted fat. Line base and side with greaseproof paper, then grease paper.

2. Cream margarine and sugar together in a bowl until light and fluffy. Beat eggs and add gradually, beating well after each addition.

Fold in flour with a metal spoon; add 1 × 15ml spoon (1 tablespoon) milk and mix lightly.

3. Place spices and custard powder in a basin. Measure treacle carefully, levelling off spoon with a knife and making sure there is none on underside of spoon; add to spices in basin. Add one-third of cake mixture; mix lightly until well blended.

4. Place alternate portions of plain and spiced cake mixture in prepared cake tin. Lightly stir mixture with a metal spoon; level top of cake mixture.

5. Bake in centre of oven for 1¼ to 1½ hours. Test by pressing with the fingers. If cooked, cake should spring back, and have begun to shrink from side of tin. Leave to cool in tin for 10 minutes; turn out, remove paper and leave to cool completely on a wire rack.

6. Make frosting: Sieve icing sugar into a bowl. Place butter and sugar in a medium-sized saucepan over a low heat. Stir with a wooden spoon until mixture boils. Remove from heat; stir in 3 × 15ml spoons (3 tablespoons) milk and vanilla essence. Add to icing sugar in bowl; beat until smooth, then quickly pour over cake.

7. Spread frosting quickly over top and side of cake; swirl with a round-ended knife. Leave in a cool place to set.

Below: *Barbados swirl cake*

RASPBERRY AND CHOCOLATE CAKE

125g (5oz) self-raising flour
25g (1oz) cocoa
100g (1oz) margarine
75g (3oz) castor sugar
4×15ml spoons (4 level
    tablespoons) raspberry jam
2 eggs
1×15ml spoon (1 tablespoon)
    milk

Filling

100g (4oz) icing sugar
50g (2oz) butter
2×15ml spoons (2 level
    tablespoons) raspberry jam

Feather Icing

150g (5oz) icing sugar
Hot water
Red food colouring

1. Prepare a moderate oven (190 deg C, 375 deg F, Gas Mark 5). Brush 2 18cm (7in) sandwich tins with oil or melted fat. Line base of each with greaseproof paper then grease paper.
2. Sift flour and cocoa together.
3. Cream margarine, castor sugar and 4 level tablespoons jam together, until mixture is light and fluffy.
4. Beat eggs and add, a little at a time, beating well after each addition. Fold sifted flour into creamed mixture, with the milk, to make a soft dropping consistency.
5. Spread mixture evenly in tins; level tops with back of spoon. Bake in centre of oven for 25 minutes. Test by pressing with the fingers. If cooked, cakes should spring back, have stopped bubbling and have begun to shrink from sides of tins. Turn out, remove paper and leave to cool completely on a wire rack.
6. To make filling: Sieve 100g (4oz) icing sugar into a bowl. Add butter and 2 × 15ml spoons (2 level tablespoons) jam; beat together until light and fluffy. Sandwich cakes together with filling.
7. To feather-ice cake: Make a paper piping bag from a triangle of greaseproof paper. Sieve 150g (5oz) icing sugar into a basin. Add hot water until icing thickly coats back of spoon (about 3 × 5ml spoons, 1½ tablespoons). Measure off 1 tablespoon icing into a small basin and colour a deep red with a little food colouring. Pour into piping bag and fold down top. Spread remaining white icing on top of cake.
8. Snip point from end of piping bag; pipe parallel lines of red icing, 1cm (½in) apart, across cake.
9. While icing is still soft, draw a pointed knife or skewer across piped lines, at 1cm (½in) intervals, each in the opposite direction from previous line. Leave to set.

Below: *Raspberry and chocolate cake*

HAZELNUT MERINGUE GATEAU

For 6 to 8 portions

Cake

100g (4oz) shelled hazelnuts
4 egg whites
250g (9oz) castor sugar
1 × 2·5ml spoon (½ teaspoon)
    vinegar
½ × 2·5ml spoon (¼ teaspoon)
    vanilla essence

Filling

1 425g (15oz) can apricots
1 142ml (5 fluid oz) carton
    double cream

1 medium-sized lemon

1. Prepare a moderate oven (200 deg C, 375 deg F, Gas Mark 5). Brush two 20·5cm (8in) sandwich tins with melted fat. Line bases and sides with greaseproof paper; grease paper.
2. Place hazelnuts on a baking sheet; bake in centre of oven for 15 to 20 minutes or until deep golden brown. Rub off skins; reserve 8 nuts for decoration. Chop remaining nuts finely.
3. Place egg whites in a clean, greasefree bowl; whisk until stiff, but not dry. Add sugar gradually, whisking well after each addition. When mixture is very stiff, whisk in vinegar and vanilla essence.
4. Fold in chopped nuts, cutting through mixture with a metal spoon, until all nuts have been incorporated. Divide mixture between prepared tins; level tops with back of a metal spoon. Bake in centre of oven for 25 to 40 minutes, or until firm to the touch.
5. Leave in tins to cool completely. Turn out on to a wire rack; remove paper.
6. Drain apricots; reserve syrup for sauce. Press apricots through a nylon sieve with a wooden spoon (or liquidise in an electric blender) to make a purée.
7. Pour cream in a basin; whisk until just stiff. Place 2 rounded tablespoons cream into a nylon piping bag, fitted with a medium-sized star tube. Carefully fold 3 rounded tablespoons apricot purée into remaining cream for filling.
8. Sandwich cakes together with filling. Pipe 8 whirls of cream on top edge of gateau; place a reserved hazelnut on each whirl. Place gateau on a serving dish.
9. To make sauce: add reserved syrup to remaining apricot purée. Scrub lemon; grate rind and squeeze juice. Add to sauce and stir well; pour into a serving jug.

Note: This gateau improves if kept overnight in refrigerator before serving.

Below: *Hazelnut meringue gateau*

CARAMEL CHOUX GATEAU
For 6 to 8 portions

Choux pastry
50g (2oz) margarine
50g (2½oz) plain flour
2 eggs

Base
150g (6oz) plain flour
50g (2oz) castor sugar
100g (4oz) soft margarine
40g (2oz) white grapes
50g (2oz) black grapes
150g (6oz) granulated sugar
1 (142ml/5 fluid oz) carton
  double cream
1 (142ml/5 fluid oz) carton
  single cream
1 × 15ml spoon (1 level
  tablespoon) castor sugar

Above: *Caramel choux gateau*

1. Prepare a moderately hot oven (200 deg C, 400 deg F, Gas Mark 6). Brush a baking sheet with melted fat or oil.
2. Place 125ml (¼ pint) water and 50g (2oz) margarine in a medium-sized saucepan; bring to boil. Remove from heat, add flour all at once and beat until mixture leaves side of pan. If mixture does not leave side of pan, return saucepan to a low heat and beat continuously with a wooden spoon, until mixture leaves side of pan. Remove from heat; leave to cool slightly.
3. Beat eggs; add to mixture, a little at a time, beating well after each addition.
4. Place mixture in a nylon piping bag fitted with a small plain tube. Pipe about 30 small balls of mixture on to baking sheet.
5. Bake in centre of oven for 30 to 35 minutes, until balls are crisp and golden brown. Remove from oven, slit each ball; leave to cool on wire rack.
6. Reduce oven temperature to cool (170 deg C, 325 deg F, Gas Mark 3). Brush a baking sheet and a 20cm (8in) fluted flan ring with melted fat or oil.
7. To make base: place flour and castor sugar in a bowl. Add margarine, cut into small pieces and rub in with the fingertips until mixture begins to stick together. Place mixture in flan ring; press down evenly and level top with the back of a metal spoon.
8. Bake in centre of oven for 35 to 40 minutes, until shortbread is lightly browned. Leave to cool on baking sheet; remove flan ring.
9. Wash grapes; cut in halves and remove pips.
10. Place granulated sugar and 125ml (¼ pint) water in a medium-sized saucepan. Heat gently until sugar has dissolved; boil rapidly for 6 to 8 minutes, until syrup turns a rich golden brown. Remove from heat; wait until bubbles subside.
11. Place a choux ball on the end of a skewer; carefully dip into caramel, to coat top. Repeat until all choux balls are coated. Leave to cool on a wire rack, caramel tops uppermost.
12. Place double and single cream and 1 level tablespoon castor sugar in a bowl; whisk until cream just holds its shape. Place three-quarters of cream in a nylon piping bag fitted with a small star tube.
13. Add grapes to remaining cream in bowl and fold in carefully. Pile cream and grapes in centre of shortbread base.
14. Pipe some cream into each choux ball. Arrange a circle of choux balls on base, around filling. Pile remaining balls in centre, to form a pyramid. Pipe remaining cream in between choux balls, to decorate. Keep in a cool place until ready to serve.

ORANGE JAPONAISE GATEAU

Cake
Grated rind of half an orange
50g (2oz) soft margarine
50g (2oz) castor sugar
50g (2oz) self-raising flour
1 × 2·5ml spoon (½ level teaspoon) baking powder
1 egg

Japonaise
2 egg whites
100g (4oz) castor sugar
75g (3oz) ground almonds

Orange Syrup
Juice of one orange
75g (3oz) granulated sugar

Orange Icing
Grated rind of half an orange
2 egg yolks
50g (2oz) granulated sugar
125g (5oz) butter

Decoration
25g (1oz) plain chocolate
1 medium-sized orange

---

1. Prepare a cool oven (170 deg C, 325 deg F, Gas Mark 3). Brush an 18cm (7in) round sandwich tin with melted fat or oil.

2. Place orange rind in a bowl. Add margarine, castor sugar, flour, baking powder and eggs. Mix together with a wooden spoon; beat for 1 to 2 minutes, until well blended.

3. Place mixture in tin; level top with back of a metal spoon. Bake in centre of oven for 20 to 25 minutes. Test cake by pressing with the fingers. If cooked, cake should spring back and have begun to shrink from side of tin. Leave cake to cool in tin for 5 minutes. Loosen edge with a round-ended knife. Turn out and leave to cool completely on a wire rack.

4. Meanwhile, make japonaise: Place oven shelves in coolest part of oven; reduce oven temperature to cool (150 deg C, 300 deg F, Gas Mark 2). Line baking sheets with silicone-treated paper. Draw a 20cm (8in) circle on each piece of paper, using a sandwich tin or saucepan lid as a guide.

5. Place egg whites in a clean, grease-free bowl. Whisk until stiff, but not dry. Whisk in half the sugar, then fold in remainder, with the ground almonds, using a metal spoon, until all the sugar and almonds have been incorporated. Divide mixture between the 2 circles and spread inside marked lines with a palette knife.

6. Bake in centre of oven for 30 to 35 minutes, when japonais should be lightly browned and firm. After 15 minutes' cooking time, lightly mark on top of each japonaise a 17·5cm (7in) circle, using a tin or saucepan lid as a guide. Mark one japonaise into 8 wedges, using a sharp knife.

7. Leave to cool on baking sheets for 10 minutes, then remove paper. Trim each japonaise to 17·5cm (7in) marked circle; cut one japonaise into 8 wedges. Place trimmings between 2 sheets of grease-proof paper; crush trimmings with a rolling pin.

8. To make orange syrup: Place juice in a measuring jug and make up to 125ml (¼ pint) with water. Place in a medium-sized saucepan with granulated sugar.

9. Heat until sugar has dissolved. Boil for 1 minute; leave to cool.

10. To make orange icing: Place orange rind in a basin, with egg yolks. Place 6 × 15ml spoons (6 tablespoons) water and 50g (2oz) granulated sugar in a small saucepan; heat slowly until sugar has dissolved. Increase heat; boil syrup for 4 minutes. Remove saucepan from heat; place a little syrup on the backs of 2 teaspoons. Press spoons together and pull apart. If a thread forms between spoons, syrup is ready. If syrup does not form a thread, return saucepan to heat and boil for a further 1 to 2 minutes; alternatively, boil until syrup registers 105 deg C (220 deg F) on a sugar thermometer.

11. Gradually whisk sugar syrup into egg mixture; continue whisking until cold. Cut butter into small pieces and whisk into egg mixture, a little at a time, whisking well after each addition.

12. Place cake on a wire rack over a plate; spoon syrup over cake; leave for 10 minutes. Spoon remaining syrup from plate over cake, until all syrup has been absorbed.

13. Divide orange icing into 2 equal portions; spread the underside of the uncut japonaise layer with half of one portion of icing. Place, spread side uppermost, on a board and place soaked cake on top.

14. Spread side of cake with remaining half portion of icing, to coat evenly. Using a palette knife, press japonaise crumbs on to side of cake, to coate evenly.

15. Place all but 2 × 15ml spoons (2 tablespoons) of remaining portion of icing in a piping bag fitted with a medium-sized star tube. Spread top of cake with 2 × 15ml spoons (2 tablespoons) icing to evenly cover top. Pipe 8 lines of icing, radiating from centre, and a row of stars around top edge.

HAZELNUT AMBER GATEAU
For 6 to 8 portions

Cake
100g (4oz) hazelnuts
3 eggs
75g (3oz) castor sugar
50g (2oz) plain flour
1 × 2·5ml spoon (½ level teaspoon) baking powder

Chocolate Meringue Icing
2 egg whites
100g (4oz) icing sugar
125g (5oz) butter
50g (2oz) plain chocolate

Caramel
150g (6oz) granulated sugar

---

1. Prepare a moderate grill; remove rack from grill pan. Place hazelnuts in grill pan; grill until nuts are a deep golden brown. Rub off skins; reserve 12 nuts for decoration. Chop 25g (1oz) nuts very finely; coarsely chop remainder.

2. Prepare a moderate oven (180 deg C, 350 deg F, Gas Mark 4). Brush 2 × 20cm (8in) sandwich tins with melted fat. Line bases with greaseproof paper; grease paper.

3. Bring a saucepan of water to the boil; remove from heat.

4. Place eggs and castor sugar in a bowl; place bowl over saucepan and whisk until mixture becomes thick and leaves a trail when whisk is lifted. Remove bowl from saucepan and continue whisking until mixture is cool.

5. Sift flour and baking powder together, then carefully fold into egg mixture with 25g (1oz) finely chopped hazelnuts, using a metal spoon.

6. Pour mixture equally into prepared tins; shake gently, to level mixture. Bake in centre of oven for 25 to 30 minutes. Test cakes by pressing with the fingers. If cooked, cakes should spring back and have begun to shrink from sides of tins.

7. Loosen edges of cakes with a round-ended knife. Turn out cakes, remove paper and leave cakes to cool on a wire rack.

8. To make chocolate meringue icing: Return saucepan of water to the boil; remove from heat.

9. Place egg whites in a clean, grease-free bowl; sieve icing sugar into bowl. Place bowl over saucepan of hot water; whisk until mixture is thick and leaves a trail when whisk is lifted. Remove bowl from saucepan and continue to whisk until mixture is cool.

10. Place butter in a bowl; beat with a wooden spoon until light and fluffy.

11. Place chocolate in a dry basin over a saucepan of hot, but not boiling, water. Stir occasionally until chocolate has melted; remove basin from saucepan.

12. Beat meringue mixture into butter, a little at a time, until all the meringue has been incorporated. Add chocolate and fold in with a metal spoon, until evenly blended.

13. Using a sharp knife, cut each cake horizontally in half. Place one top layer on a wire rack over a plate.

14. To make caramel: Place granulated sugar and 6 × 15ml spoons (6 tablespoons) water in a medium-sized saucepan. Heat gently until sugar has dissolved; boil rapidly for 6 to 8 minutes, until syrup has turned a rich golden brown. Remove from heat and allow bubbles to subside.

15. Pour over sponge layer on wire rack; spread over surface, using a palette knife. While caramel is still hot, using an oiled knife, mark into 8 equal-sized wedges.

16. Place 2 × 15ml spoons (1 rounded tablespoon) icing into a piping bag fitted with a small star tube. Reserve half of remaining icing for side of gateau.

17. Spread one layer of sponge with one-third of icing, place second layer on top and continue layering, ending with a layer of icing. Top with caramel-covered layer of sponge.

18. Spread side of gateau with reserved icing. Place coarsely-chopped hazelnuts on a piece of greaseproof paper and press on to side of gateau with a palette knife.

19. Pipe 24 swirls of icing around top edge of gateau; arrange reserved hazelnuts on alternate swirls of icing. Chill until ready to serve.

Right, clockwise from top: *Hazelnut amber gateau, orange japonaise gateau, roseberry gateau*

ROSEBERRY MERINGUE GATEAU

3 egg whites
175g (6oz) icing sugar

Filling
150g (6oz) plain chocolate
8 rose leaves with stalks
¼kg (8oz) raspberries
25g (1oz) castor sugar
1 170ml (6 fluid oz) carton double cream
1 142ml (5 fluid oz) carton single cream

1. Heat oven at lowest setting. Place a sheet of greaseproof paper on each of 2 baking sheets. Draw two 18cm (7in) circles on one baking sheet and one circle on the other; invert paper and brush marked circles with oil. (Alternatively, use silicone-treated paper and omit oil).

2. Half-fill a saucepan with water; boil, then remove from heat.

3. Place egg whites in a clean, greasefree bowl. Sieve icing sugar into bowl. Place bowl over saucepan of hot water; whisk until mixture is thick and leaves a trail when whisk is lifted. Remove bowl from saucepan and continue whisking until mixture is cool.

4. Divide meringue between 3 circles. Spread to inside of marked lines; smooth tops.

5. Place baking sheets on shelves below centre of oven for 3 to 4 hours. Meringue rounds should lift off paper easily. When meringues are cold, store in a tin until required.

6. Break up chocolate and place in a dry basin over a saucepan of hot, but not boiling, water. Stir occasionally until chocolate has melted; remove basin from saucepan.

7. Wash and dry rose leaves. Draw underside of leaves over surface of chocolate. Drain off excess chocolate and place leaves, chocolate sides uppermost, on a piece of waxed or greaseproof paper. Leave to set in the refrigerator for about 30 minutes.

8. Spread base of each meringue round with remaining melted chocolate. Leave rounds to dry, chocolate sides uppermost, on a wire rack.

9. Reserve 5 raspberries for decoration; place remainder in a bowl with castor sugar and stir gently. Cover and leave for about 30 minutes.

10. Place double and single cream in a bowl; whisk until cream just holds its shape. Place 2 rounded tablespoons cream in a piping bag fitted with a medium-sized star tube.

11. Add raspberries and juice to remaining cream and fold in carefully.

12. Place one layer of meringue on a serving plate, chocolate side downwards. Spread with half the raspberry mixture. Cover with another meringue layer and spread with remaining raspberry mixture. Top with remaining meringue round and pipe 8 swirls of cream around top edge, with 8 small stars in between.

13. Pipe another 10 small stars of cream, in a circle, in the centre. Place a reserved raspberry on alternate stars.

14. Peel rose leaves from chocolate and arrange a chocolate leaf on each small star of cream at edge.

13. Leave gateau in refrigerator for up to 3 hours before serving.

Small Cakes

CHOCOLATE TRUFFLE SLICES
Makes 12

Base
100g (4oz) plain flour
½ × 2·5ml spoon (¼ level teaspoon) salt
50g (2oz) margarine
25g (1oz) castor sugar
Cold water to mix

Filling
200g (8oz) plain cake
75g (3oz) icing sugar
25g (1oz) glacé cherries
25g (1oz) mixed dried fruit
25g (1oz) cut mixed peel
2 × 15ml spoons (2 level tablespoons) cocoa

Topping
25g (1oz) cocoa
25g (1oz) castor sugar
3 drops corn oil

1. Prepare a moderate oven (180 deg C, 350 deg F, Gas Mark 4).
2. Brush a shallow, 18cm (7in) square tin with melted fat or oil.
3. Place flour and salt in a bowl; add margarine, cut into small pieces and rub in with the fingertips until mixture resembles fine breadcrumbs. Stir in sugar.
4. Add sufficient water and mix with a fork, to form a firm dough. Turn out on to a floured board and knead lightly.
5. Roll out dough and trim to an 18cm (7in) square. Place in tin; prick all over with a fork.
6. Bake just above centre of oven for 20 minutes, until lightly browned; leave to cool in tin.
7. To make filling: Crumble cake and sieve icing sugar into a mixing bowl. Coarsely chop cherries; add to bowl with mixed dried fruit and peel.
8. Place 2 × 15ml spoons (2 level tablespoons) cocoa in a saucepan; pan; add 6 × 15ml spoons (6 tablespoons) water and bring to boil, stirring with a wooden spoon; remove from heat.
9. Stir dry mixture into saucepan and beat with a wooden spoon until smooth. Spread mixture on to pastry base in tin. Leave to cool, then chill in refrigerator for 30 minutes.
10. To make topping: Place 25g (1oz) cocoa, sugar, 3 × 15ml spoons (3 tablespoons) water and oil in a saucepan; bring to boil, stirring continuously with a wooden spoon. Cook for 1 to 2 minutes, until mixture becomes thick and creamy.
11. Pour topping on to filling and quickly spread with a rounded-ended knife.
12. When topping has set, cut in half and cut each half into 6 slices.

COCONUT AND RAISIN COOKIES
Makes 9

Filling
25g (1oz) margarine
5 × 15ml spoons (5 level tablespoons) golden syrup
50g (1½oz) desiccated coconut
50g (1½oz) seedless raisins

Base
150g (4oz) self-raising flour
½ × 2·5ml (¼ level teaspoon) salt
75g (2oz) margarine
75g (2oz) castor sugar
1 egg

Topping
Icing sugar

Left, clockwise from top: Coconut and raisin cookies, hazelnut shortbread, cherry and almond crunch, chocolate truffle slices

1. Prepare a moderate oven (180 deg C, 350 deg F, Gas Mark 4). Brush a shallow, 18cm (7in) square tin with melted fat or oil. Line base of tin with greaseproof paper; grease paper.
2. To prepare filling: Place margarine in a small saucepan. Measure golden syrup carefully, levelling off spoon with a knife and making sure there is none on underside of spoon; add to saucepan, with desiccated coconut and raisins.
3. Heat gently, stirring with a wooden spoon, until margarine has melted and ingredients are well mixed. Remove from heat; leave to cool.
4. To prepare base: Place flour and salt in a bowl. Add margarine, cut into small pieces and rub in with the fingertips until mixture resembles fine breadcrumbs. Stir in sugar.
5. Beat egg; add to bowl and mix with a fork, to form a firm dough.
6. Turn out on to a floured board and knead lightly; cut in half. Roll out each piece of dough to an 18cm (7in) square and trim to fit tin.
7. Place one piece of dough in tin, spread filling over and cover with remaining piece of dough.
8. Bake just above centre of oven for 20 to 25 minutes, until lightly browned.
9. Leave cookies to cool in tin for 5 minutes; turn out, remove paper and leave to cool completely on a wire rack. Dredge lightly with icing sugar and cut into 9 squares.

ALMOND AND CHERRY CRUNCH

Makes 18 triangles

Base

150g (6oz) self-raising flour
75g (3oz) margarine
75g (3oz) castor sugar
1 egg

Topping

50g (2oz) flaked almonds
25g (1oz) glacé cherries
25g (1oz) margarine
2×15ml spoons (2 tablespoons) evaporated milk
175g (7oz) icing sugar

1. Prepare a moderate oven (180 deg C, 350 deg F, Gas Mark 4).
2. Brush a shallow 18cm (7in) square tin with melted fat or oil. Line base of tin with greaseproof paper; grease paper.
3. Place flour in a bowl. Add margarine, cut into small pieces and rub in with the fingertips until mixture resembles fine breadcrumbs; stir in castor sugar.
4. Beat egg and add to mixture; mix with a fork, to form a firm dough.

5. Press mixture in tin; level top with back of a metal spoon. Bake in centre of oven for 15 to 20 minutes, until lightly browned at edges.
6. Leave pastry to cool in tin for 15 minutes; turn out, remove paper and leave to cool completely on a wire rack.
7. Make topping. Prepare a moderate grill; remove rack from grill pan. Place flaked almonds in grill pan; toast until deep, golden brown.
8. Roughly chop cherries. Place 25g (1oz) margarine and evaporated milk in small saucepan; heat gently until margarine has melted; then remove from heat.
9. Sieve icing sugar into saucepan; beat with a wooden spoon until smooth.
10. Place topping on crunch base. Spread to edges with a palette knife; press almonds and cherries on to topping.
11. When icing has set, cut into 9 squares and cut each square in half, to form 2 triangles.

HAZELNUT SHORTBREAD

50g (2oz) shelled hazelnuts
150g (6oz) plain flour
50g (2oz) castor sugar
100g (4oz) margarine

1. Prepare a moderate oven (180 deg C, 350 deg F, Gas Mark 4).
2. Prepare a moderate grill; remove rack from grill pan. Place hazelnuts in grill pan; grill until deep golden brown. Rub off skins; chop nuts very finely.
3. Brush a shallow, 18cm (7in) square tin with melted fat or oil.
4. Place flour and sugar in a bowl. Add margarine, cut into small pieces and rub in with the fingertips until mixture begins to bind together; stir in nuts.
5. Spread mixture in tin; level top

with back of a metal spoon. Bake in centre of oven for 20 minutes, until shortbread is lightly browned at edges.
6. Leave to cool in tin for 15 minutes. Turn out, remove paper and leave to cool completely on a wire rack. Place on a board. Cut in half and cut each half into 8 bars.

SINGIN' HINNY

200g (8oz) plain flour
½×2·5ml spoon (¼ level teaspoon) bicarbonate of soda
1×2·5ml spoon (½ level teaspoon) cream of tartar
1×2·5ml spoon (½ level teaspoon) salt
75g (3oz) lard
75g (3oz) currants
Milk

1. Lightly grease a large thick-based frying pan.
2. Sift flour, bicarbonate of soda, cream of tartar and salt into a bowl. Add lard, cut into small pieces, and rub in with the fingertips until

50

mixture resembles fine bread-crumbs. Add currants and about 4 × 15ml spoons (6 tablespoons) milk; stir with a fork until just mixed to a soft dough. Place frying pan over low heat.

3. Turn out dough on to a floured board and knead lightly. Roll out to a circle 20cm (8in) in diameter. Place in frying pan and cook until golden brown on underside, about 15 minutes. Turn with a fish slice; lightly press down edge with the slice, and cook on other side for a further 8 to 10 minutes.

4. Remove from pan. Split in half with a sharp knife and spread one half with butter. Sandwich together and cut into wedges. Serve hot.

Below: *Singin' Hinnies*

MOCHA CRUNCH
Makes 18

Base
150g (6oz) plain flour
50g (2oz) castor sugar
100g (4oz) butter or margarine

Topping
2 × 15ml spoons (2 level
   tablespoons) clear honey
50g (2oz) plain chocolate
100g (4oz) margarine
1 × 5ml spoon (1 level teaspoon)
   instant coffee
75g (3oz) cornflakes
75g (3oz) seedless raisins

1. Prepare a cool oven (170 deg C, 325 deg F, Gas Mark 3).
2. Brush a shallow, 18cm (7in) square tin with melted fat or oil.
3. Place flour and sugar in a bowl. Add 100g (4oz) butter or margarine, cut into small pieces and rub in with the fingertips until mixture begins to stick together.

Above: *Mocha crunch*

4. Place mixture in tin. Level top with back of a metal spoon; press down lightly.
5. Bake in centre of oven for 30 to 35 minutes, until shortbread is lightly browned at edges. Leave to cool in tin.
6. To make topping: Measure honey carefully, levelling off spoon with a knife and making sure there is none on underside of spoon. Place in a large saucepan, with chocolate, 100g (4oz) margarine and instant coffee.
7. Heat gently, stirring continuously, until margarine and chocolate have melted and ingredients are well mixed; bring to boil, remove from heat and leave to cool.
8. Stir in cornflakes and raisins, until coated in chocolate mixture.
9. Spread on to shortbread base and leave in refrigerator until set. When set, cut into 3 and cut each third into 6 bars.

MERINGUES
Makes 6

2 egg whites
100g (4oz) castor sugar
1 × 142ml (5 fluid oz) carton
  double cream

1. Heat oven at lowest setting; place a shelf in coolest part.
2. Line a baking sheet with grease-proof paper and brush lightly with oil.
3. Place egg whites in a clean, grease-free bowl. Whisk until stiff, but not dry. Whisk in half the sugar, then fold in remainder, cutting through mixture with a metal spoon until all sugar has been incorporated.
4. Fill a tablespoon with meringue and smooth it into a mound from each side with a knife. Hold side of spoon on baking sheet and care- fully scoop the meringue off with another tablespoon. Repeat pro- cedure to make 12 shells. Place in coolest part of oven for 3 to 4 hours. Meringues should lift off paper easily. When meringues are cold, store in a tin until required.
5. Place cream in a basin; whisk until just thick. Sandwich merin- gues together with cream and place them in paper cake cases.

Variations :
Use basic recipe and spread or pipe 2 × 15cm (8in) circles on to greased paper. (Shape tiny merin- gue shells with any excess mixture). Dry out, then layer with fruit and whipped cream. One 5ml spoon (1 level teaspoon) instant coffee may be added to sugar before whisking into egg whites.

Below: *Meringues*

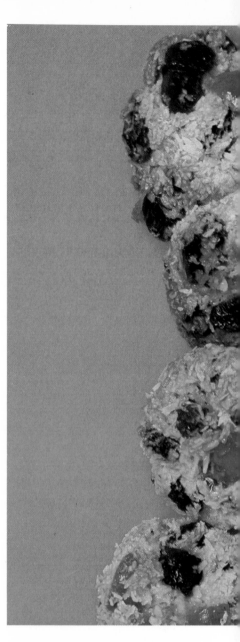

TUTTI-FRUTTI COOKIES
Makes about 20

50g (2oz) glacé cherries
25g (1oz) walnuts (optional)
100g (4oz) sultanas
50g (2oz) seedless raisins
100g (4oz) desiccated coconut
1 small can sweetened condensed
  milk

1. Prepare a moderate oven (190 deg C, 375 deg F, Gas Mark 5). Grease 2 baking sheets.
2. Cut cherries into quarters. Chop the walnuts, if used. Place cherries, walnuts, sultanas, raisins, 50g (2oz) coconut and condensed milk in a bowl and mix together.

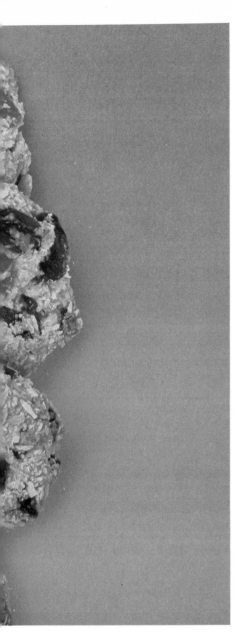

OATY-TOPPED SQUARES

100g (4oz) margarine
100g (4oz) castor sugar
2 eggs
100g (4oz) self-raising flour

Topping
50g (2oz) glacé cherries
2×15ml spoons (2 level
    tablespoons) golden syrup
75g (3oz) margarine
50g (2oz) seedless raisins
75g (3oz) demerara sugar
75g (3oz) rolled (porridge) oats

1. Prepare a cool oven (170 deg C, 325 deg F, Gas Mark 3). Brush a 28cm × 18cm × 4cm deep (11in × 7in × 1½in) tin with oil or melted fat and line with greaseproof paper.
2. Cream margarine and castor sugar together until light and fluffy.
3. Beat eggs; add gradually, beating well after each addition. Fold in flour, using a metal spoon. Spread in tin and level top with back of spoon.
4. Cut cherries into quarters. Measure golden syrup carefully, levelling off spoon with a knife, and making sure there is none on the underside of spoon. Place in a saucepan with margarine; melt over a low heat. Add remaining ingredients, mix well. Spread over cake mixture.
5. Bake just above the centre of the oven for 35 to 50 minutes. Test by pressing with the fingers. If cooked, cake should spring back and have begun to shrink from sides of tin. Leave to cool in tin; turn out, remove paper and place on a board. Cut into 18 squares.

Note: For a hot pudding, serve immediately after baking, with custard or cream.

Below: *Oaty-topped squares*

Above: *Tutti-frutti cookies*

3. Take heaped teaspoonsful of the mixture; form into about 20 small balls with the hands. Place remaining coconut on a plate and roll balls of mixture in coconut, to coat. Place on baking sheets; press lightly with a fork, to flatten slightly.
4. Bake in centre of oven for 7 to 10 minutes, until golden brown and crisp. Carefully remove from oven and leave to cool on baking sheets; carefully lift on to a cooling rack, using a palette knife. Store in an air-tight tin when cookies are cold.

CHOUX PASTRY

65g (2½oz) plain flour
50g (2oz) margarine
125ml (¼ pint) water
2 eggs

1. Measure flour on to a plate or greaseproof paper. Place margarine and water in a medium-sized saucepan, bring to boil, remove from heat. Add all the flour immediately—see picture 1; beat

*Left: Making choux pastry and eclairs.
1 to 5 from top to bottom (see recipes)*

well with a wooden spoon until mixture leaves side of the pan—see picture 2.
2. If mixture does not leave side of pan, return to a low heat and cook, beating continuously, until mixture leaves side of pan. Cool slightly.
3. Beat eggs; add to mixture a little at a time, beating well after each addition—see picture 3. The choux pastry is now ready for use. If not to be used immediately, cover with wetted greaseproof paper and a saucepan lid.

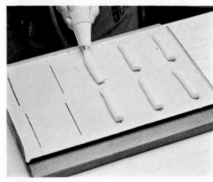

CHOCOLATE ECLAIRS
Makes 10

1 quantity choux pastry

Filling and Icing
1 × 142ml (5 fluid oz) carton
  double cream
2 × 15ml spoons (2 tablespoons)
  milk
100g (4oz) plain chocolate
1 × 5ml spoon (1 teaspoon) oil
25g (2oz) castor sugar

1. Prepare a moderately hot oven (200 deg C, 400 deg F, Gas Mark 6). Grease and flour a baking sheet. Mark 10, 10cm (4in) lines with the handle of a wooden spoon on baking sheet.
2. Make choux pastry. Place mixture in a nylon piping bag fitted with a 1·3cm (½in) plain tube, and pipe 10 lengths on to the marked lines on baking sheet—see picture 4. Alternatively, divide the mixture into 10, and smooth each to a neat shape on marked lines.
3. Bake just above centre of oven for 30 to 35 minutes until well risen, crisp and golden brown. Remove from oven and slit each along one side with a small sharp knife, to allow steam to escape. Leave to cool on a wire rack.
4. Place cream and milk in a basin and whisk until cream just holds

its shape. Fill each eclair with cream.
5. To make chocolate icing: roughly chop chocolate and place in a basin with 3 × 15ml spoons (3 tablespoons) cold water, oil and sugar. Put over a small saucepan of boiling water, and stir until chocolate has melted and mixture is smooth. Remove basin and leave to cool.
6. Hold each eclair at either end between finger and thumb and invert into chocolate icing, to coat top—see picture 5. Leave eclairs to set on a wire rack.

Note: store unfilled eclairs in a tin for up to a week. Crispen in a cool oven, if necessary, before serving.
To freeze: wrap each filled and decorated eclair in self-clinging plastic wrap. Place in a freezer bag, chill, label and freeze. Store for up to two months. *To serve:* unwrap, place on a plate and leave to thaw at room temperature for a minimum of 1 hour.

MAIDS OF HONOUR
Makes 12 to 15

570ml (1 pint) fresh milk
1×5ml spoon (1 teaspoon) rennet
    or 1 rennet tablet
25g (1oz) butter
1 egg
25g (1oz) ground almonds
1×2·5ml spoon (½ level teaspoon)
    finely grated lemon rind
25g (1oz) castor sugar
1 small (200g/7½oz) packet
    frozen puff pastry, just thawed
25g (½oz) currants

1. Make junket, using milk and rennet, but omitting sugar, as directed on bottle of rennet; leave in a warm place to set (if it does not set, move it to a warmer place). Pour into a large nylon sieve placed over a basin; cover and leave in a cool place for at least 4 hours, or overnight. This should make 125ml (¼ pint) curds; discard whey.

2. Prepare a hot oven (210 deg C, 425 deg F, Gas Mark 7). Press curds through sieve into a bowl; melt butter.

3. Beat egg and add to curds, together with ground almonds, lemon rind, sugar and butter; mix well.

4. Roll out pastry thinly on a lightly floured board. Using a cutter, 1cm (½in) larger than top measurement of tartlet tins, cut pastry into 12 to 15 rounds. Place rounds centrally over tartlet tins and ease into tins; press pastry well into base of tins, but avoid stretching pastry, or tarts will become oval on cooking.

5. Place a teaspoonful of filling into each pastry case; sprinkle a few currants on top of each.

6. Bake just above centre of oven for 20 to 25 minutes, until pale golden brown.

7. Leave in tins for a few minutes, then lift out and leave to cool on a wire rack. Serve cold.

Below: *Maids of honour*

JAM TARTS
Makes 4

Shortcrust Pastry
200g (8oz) plain flour
1 × 2·5ml spoon (½ level teaspoon)
    salt
50g (2oz) lard
50g (2oz) margarine
Cold water to mix

Jam

1. Prepare a hot oven (210 deg C, 425 deg F, Gas Mark 7).
2. Place flour and salt in a bowl. Add fats, cut into small pieces, and rub in with the fingertips until mixture resembles fine bread-crumbs.
3. Add about 2 × 15ml spoons (2 tablespoons) cold water and mix with a fork to form a firm dough. Turn out on to a floured board and knead lightly. Roll out to 3mm (⅛in) thickness.
4. Using a fluted cutter, 1cm (½in) larger than top measurement of a tartlet tin, cut out rounds of pastry firmly. Place rounds, centrally, over tartlet tins and gently ease pastry into tins; avoid stretching pastry. Press each round firmly into tin with the thumb, making sure pastry rim is evenly above the edge of tin and that it stands upright. Using a teaspoon, half fill tarts with jam.
5. Bake on shelf just above centre of oven for about 15 minutes, until pastry is pale golden brown.
6. Leave tarts in tins for a few minutes, to set jam; lift out and leave to cool on a wire rack.

Below: *Jam tarts*

Biscuits

BRANDY SNAPS
Makes 15 to 20

3×15ml spoons (3 level
   tablespoons) golden syrup
50g (2oz) margarine
50g (2oz) castor sugar
1×5ml spoon (1 teaspoon) lemon
   juice
50g (2oz) plain flour
1×5ml spoon (1 level teaspoon)
   ground ginger

---

1. Prepare a moderate oven
(180 deg C, 350 deg F, Gas Mark 4).
Lightly grease 3 baking sheets.
2. Measure golden syrup carefully, levelling off spoon with a
knife and making sure there is none
on underside of spoon. Place in a
small saucepan together with margarine, sugar and lemon juice.
Heat slowly until margarine has
melted; remove from heat.
3. Sift flour and ginger together
and stir into saucepan. Leave to
become quite cold.
4. Place 4 small teaspoonfuls of
mixture on each baking sheet, well
apart, and bake, one at a time, for
about 8 to 14 minutes, until brandy
snaps are deep golden brown.
5. Have ready a wooden spoon.
Remove baking sheet from oven,
and leave to cool for 1 minute.
Place second baking sheet in oven.
Carefully loosen brandy snaps
from first baking sheet with a
palette knife; invert one brandy
snap on to the palm of the hand,
place wooden spoon handle across

Above: Brandy snaps

the centre, then press brandy snap
over handle, pressing gently to
join the overlapping sides. Hold
until set, then gently remove from
wooden spoon; leave to cool on a
wire rack. Quickly roll remaining
brandy snaps. If the brandy snaps
have set on baking sheet and are
difficult to remove or roll, place in
oven for about 2 minutes.
6. Repeat procedure. Store the
brandy snaps in an airtight tin.

Note: The brandy snaps may be
filled with whipped cream just
before serving.

GINGERNUTS
Makes about 36

200g (8oz) self-raising flour
Pinch of salt
1 × 10ml spoon (2 level
  teaspoons) ground ginger
1 × 5ml spoon (1 level teaspoon)
  bicarbonate of soda
100g (4oz) castor sugar
1 egg
2 × 15ml spoons (2 level
  tablespoons) golden syrup
2 × 15ml spoons (2 level
  tablespoons) black treacle
75g (3oz) margarine

---

1. Prepare a cool oven (170 deg C, 325 deg F, Gas Mark 3). Lightly grease 2 baking sheets.
2. Sift flour, salt, ginger and bicarbonate of soda into a bowl: add sugar. Beat egg.
3. Measure golden syrup and black treacle carefully into a medium-

SCOTCH SHORTBREAD
Makes 2 × 16cm (6½in) shortbreads

225g (9oz) plain flour
75g (3oz) castor sugar
150g (6oz) butter

---

1. Prepare a cool oven (170 deg C, 325 deg F, Gas Mark 3). Lightly grease 2 baking sheets. Lightly brush a wooden shortbread mould with oil. Mix together 1 × 5ml spoon (1 level teaspoon) flour and 1 × 5ml spoon (1 level teaspoon) castor sugar; sprinkle over mould.
2. Place flour and sugar in a bowl. Add butter, cut into small pieces, and rub in with the fingertips until mixture resembles fine breadcrumbs. Knead in bowl until mixture holds together. Turn out on to a board and knead until smooth.
3. Cut dough into 2 equal pieces. Gently tap shortbread mould, to remove surplus flour and sugar. Place 1 piece of dough in the mould and roll across mould with a

Above: *Scotch shortbread*

rolling pin, to fill mould evenly. Invert mould over board; tap edge on board until shortbread begins to loosen around edge. Place over baking sheet and let shortbread fall out of mould, easing it out with the point of a knife, if necessary. Repeat with second piece of dough, sprinkling mould with flour and sugar, as before.
4. Bake shortbread near centre of oven, until pale golden brown, about 35 to 45 minutes. Remove from oven and leave to cool on baking sheets for 10 to 15 minutes. Carefully lift on to a wire rack, sprinkle with a little sugar and leave to cool completely. To serve, cut or break into pieces.

Note: If a shortbread mould is not available, divide dough into 2 equal pieces and roll out each piece to a 16·5cm (7in) round. Place on a baking sheet, flute edges and prick all over with a fork. Bake as directed above.

sized pan, levelling off spoon with a knife and making sure there is none on underside of spoon. Add margarine and heat until melted. Remove from heat. Gradually stir in flour mixture and egg, mix well.

4. Leave mixture to cool slightly. Form 24 heaped teaspoonsful of mixture into balls. Place 12, a little apart to allow for spreading, on each baking sheet.

5. Bake near centre of oven for 12 to 20 minutes, until golden brown. Leave to cool on baking sheets for a few minutes, then remove and leave to cool completely on a wire rack. Repeat with remaining mixture. Store in a tin.

Note: 25g (1oz) chopped walnuts, 50g (2oz) sultanas or 50g (2oz) chopped glacé cherries may be added with flour and egg to melted mixture, if desired.

Below: *Ginger nuts*

CHOCOLATE COOKIES
Makes 18

Above: *Chocolate cookies*

1st layer
100g (4oz) margarine
50g (1½oz) castor sugar
3 × 15ml spoons (3 level tablespoons) cocoa
1 egg, beaten
1 × 5ml spoon (1 teaspoon) vanilla essence
175g (6oz) digestive biscuits
50g (2oz) walnuts

2nd layer
200g (8oz) icing sugar
2 × 15ml spoons (2 level tablespoons) custard powder
50g (2oz) soft margarine
3 × 15ml spoons (3 tablespoons) hot water

3rd layer
75g (3oz) plain chocolate
50g (1½oz) butter
50g (1½oz) icing sugar

1. Brush a 28cm by 18cm (11in by 7in) Swiss-roll tin with melted fat.

2. To make 1st layer: melt 100g (4oz) margarine, castor sugar and cocoa in a small saucepan. Add beaten egg and vanilla essence, stir for 1 minute without boiling; remove from heat. Stir in crushed biscuits and chopped walnuts. Spread mixture in tin; leave to cool completely, then chill.

3. To make 2nd layer: sift icing sugar and custard powder into a bowl; beat in margarine and hot water. Spread over biscuit layer; chill.

4. To make 3rd layer: melt chocolate with butter in a small basin over a saucepan of hot water; stir occasionally until chocolate has melted. Remove from heat; beat in icing sugar. Spread over 2nd layer; chill until firm. Serve cut into 18 squares.

EASTER BISCUITS
Makes about 18

300g (12oz) plain flour
1 × 5ml spoon (1 level teaspoon)
  baking powder
1 × 5ml spoon (1 level teaspoon)
  mixed spice
1 × 5ml spoon (1 level teaspoon)
  cinnamon
150g (6oz) butter or margarine
150g (6oz) castor sugar
100g (4oz) currants
2 eggs

---

1. Prepare a moderate oven (180 deg C, 350 deg F, Gas Mark 4). Grease 3 baking sheets.
2. Sift flour, baking powder, mixed spice and cinnamon into a bowl. Add butter or margarine, cut into small pieces, and rub in with the fingertips until mixture resembles fine breadcrumbs. Stir

in sugar and currants.
3. Beat eggs together and add to mixture, mixing with a fork to form a stiff dough.
4. Turn out on to a floured board and knead lightly. Roll out to 6mm (¼in) thickness. Cut into rounds

with a 8cm (3½in) fluted cutter.
5. Place rounds on baking sheets and bake until lightly browned, 15 to 20 minutes. Leave to cool on a wire rack.

Below: *Easter Biscuits*

ICED BISCUITS

Basic Biscuit Mixture
150g (6oz) margarine
150g (6oz) castor sugar
1 × 5ml spoon (1 teaspoon) vanilla
  essence
2 × 15ml spoons (2 tablespoons)
  milk
250g (10oz) plain flour
50g (2oz) cornflour
1 × 5ml spoon (1 level teaspoon)
  baking powder

---

1. Prepare a moderately hot oven (200 deg C, 400 deg F, Gas Mark 6). Grease 2 baking sheets.
2. Cream margarine and sugar together. Stir in remaining ingredients, then knead until mixture is smooth.
3. Roll out dough thinly; cut into 5cm (2in) squares, 5cm (2in) by 3cm (1in) oblongs and 6cm (2½in) diamonds; cut some 6cm (2½in) and 5cm (2in) rounds; cut 2cm (¾in) rounds from centres of some of the 5cm (2in) rounds.
4. Place biscuits on baking sheets; bake in centre of oven until pale

golden brown, about 8 minutes. Leave to cool on a wire rack.
5. To decorate: Sandwich the oblongs and diamonds with chocolate spread or coffee butter icing; decorate with white glacé icing or coffee butter icing and walnuts or chocolate vermicelli. Ice 6cm (2½in) rounds with pink glacé icing; top with glacé cherries.

Sandwich some whole 5cm (2in) rounds with jam: decorate with white glacé icing and glacé cherries. Decorate squares with red jam, coconut and glacé cherries. Spread other whole 5cm (2in) rounds with red or green jam or lemon curd; place cut rings on top.

Below: *Iced biscuits*

Index